P9-CCR-842

Kansas City, MO Public Library

00001187914437

FINISH *the* FIGHT!

THE BRAVE AND REVOLUTIONARY WOMEN
WHO FOUGHT FOR THE RIGHT TO VOTE

FINISH *the* FIGHT!

THE BRAVE AND REVOLUTIONARY WOMEN
WHO FOUGHT FOR THE RIGHT TO VOTE

1920

WRITTEN BY THE STAFF OF THE NEW YORK TIMES, INCLUDING VERONICA CHAMBERS,
JENNIFER SCHUESSLER, AMISHA PADNANI, JENNIFER HARLAN,
SANDRA E. GARCIA, AND VIVIAN WANG

PORTRAIT ILLUSTRATIONS BY

Monica Ahanonu, Rachelle Baker, Kristen Buchholz, Alex Cabal, Noa Denmon, Ellen Duda,
Shyama Golden, Johnalynn Holland, Hillary Kempenich, Nhung Lê, Ella Trujillo, and Steffi Walthall

VERSIFY | HOUGHTON MIFFLIN HARCOURT | BOSTON NEW YORK

Copyright © 2020 by The New York Times Company

All rights reserved. For information about permission to reproduce selections from this book, write to trade.permissions@hmhco.com or to Permissions, Houghton Mifflin Harcourt Publishing Company, 3 Park Avenue, 19th Floor, New York, New York 10016.

Versify® is an imprint of Houghton Mifflin Harcourt Publishing Company. Versify is a registered trademark of Houghton Mifflin Harcourt Publishing Company.

hmhbooks.com

Illustration credits: Trading Cards, pp. viii–xi; Why It Matters, p. xii; The Votes for Women Game, pp. 80–81; Suffrage Forest, p. 121 © Ellen Duda • Frances Ellen Watkins Harper, p. 18 © Steffi Walthall • Josephine St. Pierre Ruffin, p. 26 © Monica Ahanonu • Elizabeth Piper Ensley, p. 34 © Rachelle Baker • Mary Church Terrell, p. 40 © Johnalynn Holland • Angelina Weld Grimké and Mary Burrill, p. 46 © Kristen Buchholz • Mabel Ping-Hua Lee, p. 54 © Nhung Lê • Ida B. Wells-Barnett, p. 60 © Shyama Golden • Jovita Idár, p. 72 © Alex Cabal • Juno Frankie Pierce, p. 82 © Noa Denmon • Susette La Flesche Tibbles, p. 88 © Ella Trujillo • Zitkála-Šá, p. 94 © Hillary Kempenich

The text was set in Athelas.
The display type was set in Mr Eaves Sans.
Cover design by Whitney Leader-Picone
Interior design by Ellen Duda
Art direction by Whitney Leader-Picone

The Library of Congress Cataloging-in-Publication data is available.

ISBN: 978-0-358-40830-7

Manufactured in the United States of America
DOC 10 9 8 7 6 5 4 3 2 1
4500800890

*We dedicate this book, with gratitude,
to the generations of women journalists who
made suffrage and equal rights their beat.*

CONTENTS

Here are some suffragists you may have learned about . . .

SUSAN B. ANTHONY

VOTES FOR WOMEN!

ELIZABETH CADY STANTON

VOTES FOR WOMEN!

MATILDA JOSLYN GAGE

VOTES FOR WOMEN!

EMMELINE PANKHURST

VOTES FOR WOMEN!

LUCY STONE

VOTES FOR WOMEN!

LUCRETIA MOTT

VOTES FOR WOMEN!

ALICE PAUL

VOTES FOR WOMEN!

CARRIE CHAPMAN CATT

VOTES FOR WOMEN!

. . . but there are lots more you should know!

INTRODUCTION

THIS IS WHAT SUFFRAGE LOOKS LIKE

IT TOOK THE BETTER PART OF A CENTURY TO PASS A LAW SAYING AMERICAN women had the right to vote. Three generations of women, and their male allies, worked tirelessly to make the Nineteenth Amendment—which decreed that states could not discriminate at the polls on the basis of sex—a reality. We call the right to vote "suffrage," but for a long time, that word was a kind of shorthand for women's rights. Without the vote, suffragists argued, women had little say over their lives and their futures and certainly much less when it came to the larger political questions that shaped the nation.

The Nineteenth Amendment is a cornerstone of gender equality in our country, yet many of us know very little about the way the right to vote was won. Kate Clarke Lemay, a historian at the National Portrait Gallery in Washington, DC, and the editor of the book *Votes for Women: A Portrait of Persistence,* puts it this way: "The way we frame suffrage needs attention. It is thought to be kind of dowdy and dour, whereas in fact it is exciting and radical. A fresh way to think of it would be this: *women* staged one of the longest social reform movements *in the history of the United States.* This is not a boring history of nagging spinsters; it is a badass history of revolution staged by political geniuses."

> "*WOMEN* STAGED ONE OF THE LONGEST SOCIAL REFORM MOVEMENTS *IN THE HISTORY OF THE UNITED STATES.*
> [SUFFRAGE] IS NOT A BORING HISTORY OF NAGGING SPINSTERS; IT IS A BADASS HISTORY OF REVOLUTION STAGED BY POLITICAL GENIUSES."

Yes, suffrage history needs a makeover. But it also needs a wider lens. For a long time it has been told mainly as the story of a few famous white women, such as Elizabeth Cady Stanton and Susan B. Anthony. It's true, they were among the most important leaders of the movement in the nineteenth century. They were some of the first to call for votes for women, and they spent more than half a century tirelessly fighting for suffrage. The Nineteenth Amendment was even called the Anthony Amendment.

But there are tons of women beyond Susan and Elizabeth's demographic who helped make suffrage a reality for *all* women. African American women such as Frances Ellen Watkins Harper and Mary Church Terrell, who championed both suffrage and civil rights. Native American women such as Susette La Flesche Tibbles and Zitkála-Šá, who worked to achieve civil rights for Native people. We wanted to tell the stories of queer women like Angelina Weld Grimké, Latina women like Jovita Idár, and Asian American women like Mabel Ping-Hua Lee. They all fought for the vote as part of a broader struggle for equality, but their stories still aren't nearly as well known as they should be.

And these stories aren't just about the Nineteenth Amendment. As important as that was, it wasn't enough to guarantee that every woman, everywhere, could vote. There were still many barriers for women of color in many places. It took more laws and many more years of activism for all women to really win the right to vote—and the fight continues.

Shirley Chisholm, who—in a tribute to the suffragists—wore white on the day in 1968 when she became the first African American woman elected to Congress, reportedly said, "If they don't give you a seat at the table, bring a folding chair." We hope that this book helps set a place at the table for some of the many incredible women who played their part in the battle for suffrage and equal rights for women.

CHAPTER 1

The Haudenosaunee Model

ON JULY 14, 1848, AN ADVERTISEMENT APPEARED IN A NEWSPAPER IN SENECA Falls in upstate New York, announcing "a Convention to discuss the social, civil, and religious condition and rights of woman." A few days later, on July 19, some three hundred women and men gathered in a local church for what is often said to be the first meeting dedicated specifically to women's rights. There, after two days of impassioned conversation, one hundred people signed a document modeled on the Declaration of Independence—but adding two words to its most famous passage: "All men *and women* are created equal."

The document was known as the Declaration of Sentiments. It had been hashed out on a parlor table by a small group of women, including Elizabeth Cady Stanton and Lucretia Mott. Elizabeth was a well-to-do woman who was chafing under traditional ideas about marriage and motherhood. Lucretia was a Quaker, a member of a religious group that already had strong ideas about equality between men and women. Like many of the early suffragists, these two women were ardent abolitionists—a term for people, both black and white, who were fighting to put an end to slavery.

The fight against slavery spurred some white women to think about their own situations. Although marriage was hardly slavery, women in 1848, no matter their race, had highly unequal rights compared with men. In some states, married women were required to surrender all their property to their husbands. In a divorce, women often had no right to custody of their children. And in many places it was not illegal for their husbands to beat them.

Lucretia Mott leaving an anti-slavery meeting where a mob had gathered. Nineteenth century.

Even in the abolitionist movement, men and women weren't equal. At meetings, women often weren't allowed to speak. At one antislavery meeting in London in 1840, the women were forced to sit silently behind a curtain, which left many of them, including Elizabeth and Lucretia, fuming.

The Declaration of Sentiments, mostly written by Elizabeth, demanded total equality for women in

economics, family life, and religion. It also included a demand that women have an equal right to vote—a demand so radical that Lucretia opposed including it in the document at all, warning that it would make the Seneca Falls Convention look "ridiculous."

And many newspapers that wrote about the convention did make fun of it. One called it "the most shocking and unnatural event ever recorded in the history of womanity." The African American abolitionist Frederick Douglass—who attended the meeting and supported women's right to vote—observed that a meeting dedicated to the rights of animals would have been greeted with more respect. That's how radical the notion of women's suffrage was at the time.

But the idea of women's equality, and women voting, wasn't outrageous to everyone in 1848. In fact, some women in America already had a say in choosing their leaders—and they were living right in the convention's backyard.

The town of Seneca Falls was located in the historic territory of the Haudenosaunee, a confederacy of six Native American nations (including the Seneca Nation, which gave the town its name) stretching across what became New York State. And long before the arrival of Europeans, the Haudenosaunee, also known as the Iroquois, practiced a form of representative democracy that gave significant power to women.

Haudenosaunee society was matrilineal, meaning that the clan you belonged to depended on your mother's ancestors, not your father's. Women made decisions about the land and farmed it, too. They owned the fruits of their own labor, and they kept their own property after marriage—a right that American women had only begun to fight for. Haudenosaunee women held veto power over decisions about war and peace. The clan mothers were the ones who nominated each clan's chief, known as the *Hoyaneh*. And they had the power to remove him, too.

There were no Haudenosaunee among the three hundred or so women and men at the Seneca Falls meeting. The Haudenosaunee were citizens of their own nation, not of the United States. They lived in their own settlements and mostly spoke their own language. But some of the women and men who gathered in Seneca Falls might have known about Haudenosaunee customs—and the power of their women—from encounters in town or from newspapers, which regularly wrote about Haudenosaunee ceremonies and other events. And at least one person at the convention had even witnessed a political debate among Haudenosaunee women and men.

In June 1848, a month before the convention, Lucretia Mott was part of a group of Quakers who spent a few weeks among the Haudenosaunee of the Seneca Nation in Cattaraugus, about one hundred miles southwest of Seneca Falls. The Quakers had been involved with helping the Haudenosaunee negotiate their relationship with the US government, which had forced them from much of their land. When Lucretia visited, the Haudenosaunee were debating whether to make changes in their political system. In a letter published in a local newspaper, she wrote about observing a traditional ceremonial dance and watching as both men and women spoke during debates.

Later, as the suffrage movement grew, Native American women became powerful inspirations to some suffragists, who saw them as visionary examples of a more equal world. Among them was Matilda Joslyn Gage, who joined the women's rights movement a few years after Seneca Falls. In 1875, when she was president of the National Woman Suffrage Association, Matilda wrote a series of newspaper articles discussing the Haudenosaunee people, praising the "nearly equal" division of power between men and women in politics as well as women's "superiority in power" in the family. Matilda became so involved with the Haudenosaunee people that she received an honorary adoption into the Wolf Clan in

1893—the same year she was denied the right to vote in a school commissioner election in New York State.

To some suffragists, Native women were powerful symbols of "the matriarchate," a kind of rule by women that they believed existed across much of the world in ancient times, before men took over. But the suffragists could express this belief in condescending ways. Even as they praised Native culture, they sometimes talked about Native people as "noble savages" who were disappearing, rather than as communities that were very much present and carrying their traditions forward.

The Haudenosaunee women had their own battles. They were fighting to protect their people's independence and way of life, which wasn't about women ruling men, but about sharing responsibilities. During the nineteenth century the

Cartoon depicting suffragists and Haudenosaunee women, published in the humor magazine Puck. *1914.*

Caroline Parker Mountpleasant. Circa 1849.

Haudenosaunee, like other Native people, were under intense pressure to adopt the Christian belief system and assimilate into white American culture. In 1848, the same year as the Seneca Falls Convention, the Seneca Nation, under pressure from the United States to implement a "civilized" form of government, adopted a written constitution. The document dissolved their traditional political system and the power it granted to clan mothers. Control of land remained with the women, but voting rights were limited to men, as they were under the US Constitution. (In fact, the Seneca Nation constitution wouldn't be changed to allow women to vote in tribal elections until 1964.)

Some Haudenosaunee women—such as Caroline Parker Mountpleasant, also known as Ga-hah-no—learned to navigate between two worlds. Born around 1824, the daughter of a chief and a clan mother of the Seneca Wolf Clan on the Tonawanda Reservation, Caroline was educated at a missionary school and forced to do her lessons in English. She later became well known for her traditional beadwork. In 1878, she was publicly named *Jigonsaseh,* or "Peace Queen," a traditional title held by some of her female ancestors. Upon her death, in 1892,

The New York Times noted how Caroline had served as a kind of cultural ambassador, welcoming prominent visitors from around the world into her home.

Today, Haudenosaunee women continue to exercise their traditional decision-making power. Louise Herne is a clan mother for the Bear Clan of the Mohawk Nation. Working alongside other women, she plans ceremonies and oversees decision-making for the clan. She also nominated the current chief after consulting with the rest of the clan. "A man cannot become a leader until a woman backs him up," she said in an interview for this book. "It has to come through the voice of a woman."

To Louise, the connection between her ancestors and the suffragists is an important piece of "hidden history" that more people should know about. In 2020, she said, "We're celebrating one hundred years of the Nineteenth Amendment. But Haudenosaunee women have had political voice for a thousand."

> "WE'RE CELEBRATING ONE HUNDRED YEARS OF THE NINETEENTH AMENDMENT. BUT HAUDENOSAUNEE WOMEN HAVE HAD POLITICAL VOICE FOR A THOUSAND."

CHAPTER 2

How Bias Nearly Ruined the Suffrage Movement

AFTER THE MEETING AT SENECA FALLS, WOMEN CONTINUED TO AGITATE FOR their rights, including the right to vote. But as the Civil War approached, the movement fell into the background as suffragists—most of whom were also abolitionists—focused their attention on fighting slavery.

The Civil War began in 1861 and divided the country between the South, which seceded from the United States in order to preserve slavery, and the North, which fought to keep the country together. In 1863, Abraham Lincoln issued the Emancipation Proclamation, which declared that all enslaved people in the states at war with the Union were now free.

When the war ended in 1865, the nation began to debate how to put itself back together and change the Constitution to provide rights for formerly enslaved people. It was a dramatic remaking of American democracy—and suffragists did not want women to be left out.

In January 1866, the first of hundreds of petitions demanding universal suffrage—voting rights for all citizens, regardless of race or gender—was presented to Congress. It was signed by a number of prominent white suffragists and abolitionists, including Elizabeth Cady Stanton and Susan B. Anthony. The principle makes perfect sense today. Women are citizens, too. Why shouldn't they vote? But it was a revolutionary idea at the time.

The Fourteenth Amendment, ratified on July 9, 1868, secured citizenship for black people born in the United States but only protected the voting rights of "male citizens." While the Declaration of Independence mentioned "men," the Constitution had not. This was the first reference to gender ever included in the Constitution, a fact that worried some suffragists. "If that word 'male' be inserted," Elizabeth warned, "it will take us a century at least to get it out."

> "IF THAT WORD 'MALE' BE INSERTED, IT WILL TAKE US A CENTURY AT LEAST TO GET IT OUT."

The Fifteenth Amendment, ratified on February 3, 1870, strengthened the voting rights of black men. But again, women were left out. And some suffragists were angry.

The National Woman Suffrage Association, led by Elizabeth and Susan, refused to support the amendment. They wanted a law that would give the vote to all of America's women too, or nothing. Another suffrage group supported the amendment, arguing that women should seek the vote at the state level instead.

During those debates, some white suffragists said ugly, racist things about black men. Elizabeth, for example, argued that uneducated black men just out of slavery were inferior, and less deserving of the vote than women like herself. The amendment "creates an antagonism everywhere between educated, refined women and the lower orders of men, especially at the South," she said.

Frederick Douglass strongly supported women's suffrage, but he worried that including women in the Fifteenth Amendment would doom it. And securing voting rights for African Americans, even just for men, was a life-or-death matter.

But some African American women disagreed. Sojourner Truth, one of the most prominent civil rights advocates of her era, felt that black women's rights were just as important. "If colored men get their rights, and not colored women theirs," she said in 1867, "you see the colored men will be masters over the women and it will be just as bad as it was before." (Although considered archaic and offensive today, the term "colored" was commonly used at the time by black men and women.)

American suffragists found themselves at a crossroads. The Fifteenth Amendment had split the movement into two factions. The fierce debates, along with the racist remarks by some white suffragists who were angry at being excluded from the vote, had left wounds.

But women were still pressing forward. All over the country, some tried to cast ballots, even though the law didn't let them. In 1869, a woman named Mary Olney Brown attempted to vote in the city of Olympia, in what was then the Washington Territory. She was turned away from the polls. The next year, in Grand Mound, Washington, Mary's sister, Charlotte Olney French, and several other women tried to vote—and they succeeded.

In 1871, the African American activist Mary Ann Shadd Cary and a multiracial group of sixty women made an unsuccessful attempt to vote in Washington, DC. And in 1872, Susan B. Anthony was arrested for trying to vote in Rochester, New York. She fought the charges in court, but lost.

Women weren't just showing up at the polls. Some of them were also fighting to get on the ballot. In 1872, Victoria Woodhull, a radical activist from New York, became the first woman to run for president—on a ticket backed by the Equal Rights Party—even though, legally, she was too young to become president and wasn't allowed to vote in the election!

In 1878, the first women's suffrage amendment was introduced in Congress. There was also a big push for suffrage on the state and local levels. By 1890,

Five officers of the Women's League in Newport, Rhode Island—one of many clubs and civic groups formed by African American women in the late nineteenth century. Circa 1899.

women had won the vote in four states or territories. And in many states, women could vote in school elections.

At the same time, things were only getting harder for African Americans seeking equal rights. After the Civil War, African American men helped put as many as two thousand black politicians and civil servants in office, including in Congress. But black voters met with violent resistance across the South, and those voting rights were soon rolled back. In the late 1800s, Southern states began enacting Jim Crow laws, which reinforced white supremacy by mandating that black and white people be segregated—separating them on trains and buses; in restaurants, theaters, and schools; and pretty much anywhere else.

And suffrage groups were not necessarily any different. Organizations such as the National American Woman Suffrage Association allowed chapters in Southern states to exclude African American women, and they sometimes made political alliances with segregationist politicians in order to advance the cause.

Amid all this, African American suffragists formed their own groups. In 1880, Mary Ann Shadd Cary founded the Colored Women's Progressive Franchise in Washington. A few years later, Sarah Garnet started the Equal Suffrage League of Brooklyn. And women like Frances Ellen Watkins Harper, Josephine St. Pierre Ruffin, and Elizabeth Piper Ensley fought for a voice in a movement that often relegated them to the sidelines. For these women, the vote represented a precious opportunity to step into their power as American citizens. As the suffragist and civil rights activist Nannie Helen Burroughs wrote in 1915: "When the ballot is put into the hands of the American woman the world is going to get a correct estimate of the Negro woman. It will find her a tower of strength of which poets have never sung, orators have never spoken, and scholars have never written."

We Are All Bound Up Together

... born of a race whose inheritance

has been outrage
and wrong

... bound together in one
great bundle
of humanity.

this grand and glorious
Revolution has co

... as to learn—no man by
the color of his skin
or the curl of his ha

You white women
speak of
Rights...

I speak of Wro

CHAPTER 3

Frances Ellen Watkins Harper

Lifting Up Her Voice

IN THE LATE 1850s, FRANCES ELLEN WATKINS HARPER WAS RIDING A STREETCAR in Pennsylvania, going about her business, when the conductor approached her and said she was not welcome to a seat. Those were for white passengers. If she wanted to ride, she would have to stand up front with the driver.

Frances was furious. She wasn't getting up, not this time.

"I did not move, but kept the same seat," she later wrote in a letter to a friend that was published in *The Liberator* newspaper. "When I was about to leave, he refused my money, and I threw it down on the car floor, and got out, after I had ridden as far as I wished. Such impudence!"

That incident on the streetcar was one of many injustices Frances faced that spurred her to give a speech at the 1866 National Woman's Rights Convention that encapsulated the sentiment of black women in the suffrage movement. In it, she said, "You white women speak here of rights. I speak of wrongs."

> "I DO NOT BELIEVE THAT GIVING THE WOMAN THE BALLOT IS IMMEDIATELY GOING TO CURE ALL THE ILLS OF LIFE. . . . YOU WHITE WOMEN SPEAK HERE OF RIGHTS. I SPEAK OF WRONGS."

Although Frances became one of the most outspoken and beloved activists of her generation, it took her a while to find her voice. She was born in Baltimore in 1825 to parents who were free blacks. She was orphaned at a young age and raised by her uncle, the Reverend William Watkins, a minister and an abolitionist, who had a huge influence on her life. Young Frances met many of her uncle's abolitionist friends and learned the power of writing and giving speeches, as well as the importance of standing up and speaking out for the things you believe in.

The reverend also ran the William Watkins Academy for Negro Youth, one of the largest schools for black children in Maryland. The course work there was rigorous. Students studied the Bible, Greek, Latin, history, geography, mathematics, music,

Frontispiece for Poems *by Frances Ellen Watkins Harper. 1898.*

writing, and public speaking. Frances's uncle drilled his students again and again until they got their lessons right. But his strictness helped Frances become a great writer and a voice for the causes she cared about.

As a teenager, she went to work as a nanny for a local Quaker family who owned a bookstore. The family noticed how much Frances loved to read and write and encouraged her interest in books. Frances read voraciously, and she began to write her own poems, which were then published in newspapers. When she was about twenty, she published her first book of poetry, *Forest Leaves*.

In 1850, Frances moved to Ohio, where she taught sewing at Union Seminary, a school near Columbus run by the African Methodist Episcopal Church. Then, something shocking happened. Some years earlier, Maryland had passed a law saying that any free blacks who entered the state could be arrested and sold into slavery. Frances was horrified when she heard the story of a free man who

Title page from Forest Leaves. *Circa 1849.*

had entered the state around 1851, unaware of the new law. He was detained and eventually sold to a white man in Georgia. He reportedly died enslaved. It was unfair, unjust, and wrong. Even though Frances was happy living among books and writing, the outside world seemed to be pulling her to get involved. Her uncle and his friends were examples of how critical it was to speak up and speak out on social justice issues. She knew she had to do something, anything, to change the laws that were costing the lives of good people whose only crime was dreaming of freedom.

Now living in Philadelphia, she joined the abolitionist movement. The house she lived in was a stop on the Underground Railroad, which meant that Frances offered safe harbor to people who had escaped slavery on their quest for freedom. She started giving speeches, taking her skill with words on the page and using it to reach people in person, and she gained a reputation as a skilled orator.

The Anti-Slavery Society of Maine hired her to go on a lecture tour around the Northeast and Canada. She gave speeches alongside other abolitionists, such as Frederick Douglass. Everywhere they went, people sat up and listened when Frances spoke.

One person who saw her speak said, "Her manner is marked by dignity and composure. She is never assuming, never theatrical."

Frances also kept writing. She was one of the first African American women in the United States to publish short stories and novels.

In 1860, Frances married a man named Fenton Harper, a widower from Ohio. She gave up lecturing to focus on raising their daughter, as well as Fenton's kids from his first marriage, on a farm near Columbus that they bought using money from her books. But in 1864, Fenton died, and Frances decided to return to her activism and push for racial and gender equality.

After the Civil War, she worked in the suffrage movement alongside white suffragists like Susan B. Anthony and Elizabeth Cady Stanton, and she pushed them to think more expansively and to consider the perspective of black women. In one of her most famous speeches, at the 1866 National Woman's Rights Convention, Frances said, "We are all bound up together in one great bundle of humanity, and society cannot trample on the weakest and feeblest of its members without receiving the curse in its own soul."

She spoke forcefully against the idea that women's suffrage would solve all problems. "I do not believe that giving the woman the ballot is immediately going to cure all the ills of life," she said. And white women, she continued, would not necessarily act in the interest of black women. "I do not believe that white women are dew-drops just exhaled from the skies. I think that like men they may be divided into three classes, the good, the bad, and the indifferent. The good would vote according to their convictions and principles; the bad, as dictated by prejudice or malice; and the indifferent will

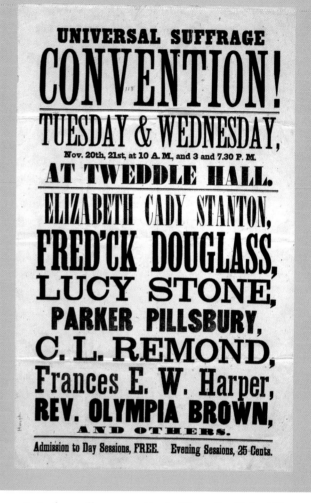

Poster for a suffrage convention in Albany, New York. 1866.

vote on the strongest side of the question, with the winning party." And then she began to tell them the story of the streetcar.

For the rest of her life, Frances continued to fight for women's rights and equal treatment for African Americans. In the 1890s, she led the American Association of Educators of Colored Youth and was a founding member of the National Association of Colored Women—alongside Mary Church Terrell and Ida B. Wells-Barnett, whom you'll learn more about later in this book. She died in 1911, less than a decade before the Nineteenth Amendment became law. Her writing, which is still read today, resonates with the intensity of someone who was born during an age of inequality but believed deeply that her country could and would change. As she wrote, "the shadows bear the promise / Of a brighter coming day."

tion of our girls.
mong our prominent progres-
women is Mrs. William E.
thews, known in the literary
as "Victoria Earle."
s. Matthews, so desirous of
what she can for her race,
a few others saw the practi-
ood of banding together well-
ing women with the hope
might in their genera-

CHAPTER 4

Josephine St. Pierre Ruffin

Spreading the Word

IN THE MID-1800s, AMERICAN WOMEN WERE STARTING TO GATHER TO TALK ABOUT the way they were treated under the law—and the ways that should change. The Seneca Falls Convention in 1848 was followed by more and more meetings across the country, where women gave rousing speeches and had intense discussions about the state of the nation. In many places, they started clubs and associations to fight for women's rights.

But all that activism meant little if nobody heard about it. There was no social media in those days, no TV or even radio. Word of mouth could only get you so far. So if the suffragists wanted to spread their message and build a community of people who would fight for change together, they had to rely on newspapers, magazines, and other print media.

Such publications as *The Lily,* started by Amelia Bloomer in 1849, and *The Una,* founded by Paulina Kellogg Wright Davis in 1853, were created to tell stories for, by, and about women. They kept those fighting for women's rights apprised of the latest developments, and they covered issues that many women cared about, from health to fashion to temperance, a movement to curtail alcohol consumption in the United States.

Many leading women's activists wrote for these publications. Elizabeth Cady Stanton wrote for both *The Una* and *The Lily*—often under the pseudonym Sunflower—and wealthy supporters of the cause helped fund them. Most of the publications were fairly short-lived. *The Una,* for example, ran for only two years before going under. There were a few exceptions: *The Woman's Journal,* which was founded by Lucy Stone and served for a time as the official publication of the National American Woman Suffrage Association (NAWSA), ran from 1870 until 1931. But even those that did manage to last hobbled along on a hodgepodge of subscriptions and the assistance of wealthy patrons. In its entire sixty-one-year run, *The Woman's Journal* did not once make a profit.

In the early 1890s, Josephine St. Pierre Ruffin started a newspaper

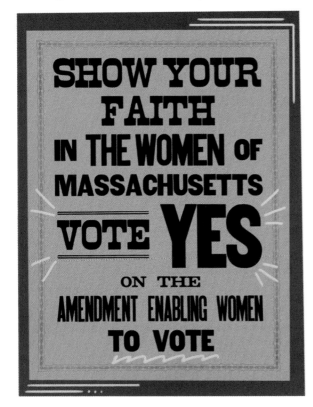

A cardboard poster for the Massachusetts Woman Suffrage Association. Circa 1915.

called *The Woman's Era*. It was the first newspaper by and for black women in the United States, and it faced an even more difficult uphill climb.

Josephine was born on August 31, 1842, in Boston. Her mother, Eliza Matilda Menhenick St. Pierre, was a white woman from Cornwall, England. Josephine's father, John St. Pierre, was from Martinique and had a mix of Native American, African, and French ancestry.

Being in an interracial marriage in the 1800s was rare: in fact, in many places it was illegal. But Massachusetts, the state where Josephine's parents lived, was very liberal when it came to interracial marriage. Massachusetts had banned slavery in the 1780s, and interracial marriage was legal there as of 1843.

But not everything in Boston was liberal. Josephine's father, a successful tailor and minister, and her mother wanted her to get the best education possible, but the public schools in Boston were segregated. Schools for black kids had far fewer resources than the ones for white children, so her parents sent her to a private grammar school for white children. Josephine had very fair skin, so at first the school assumed that she was white, like the other students. But when school officials realized she was mixed race, they expelled her.

Josephine then went to an integrated school in Salem, Massachusetts. She graduated and later attended a finishing school in Boston. A finishing school was like a high school, but instead of learning calculus, environmental science, and algebra, upper-class young women were taught manners and proper etiquette, so they would be ready for marriage and society.

When Josephine graduated, she married George Lewis Ruffin, who became the first black man to graduate from Harvard Law School. It was 1858, a year after the Supreme Court's infamous ruling in the *Dred Scott* case, which said that black people could never be American citizens, even if they were free. As soon as Josephine and George married, they boarded a ship to Liverpool, England. The

Ruffins did not want to raise their children in a country that allowed slavery, and they thought things would be better abroad.

After the outbreak of the Civil War, the Ruffins moved back to Massachusetts and bought a home. They had five children, and Josephine raised them as her husband climbed the political ranks in Boston. He served in the Massachusetts state legislature and the Boston Common Council, and later became a judge.

Meanwhile, Josephine worked with the US Sanitary Commission (an early version of the American Red Cross) and helped found the Boston Kansas Relief Association, which aided formerly enslaved people who migrated to western states to begin a new life. She also wrote for *The Courant,* a weekly newspaper that covered the African American community, and joined the New England Woman's Press Association.

George died suddenly in 1886 and left Josephine widowed at the age of forty-four.

She hadn't stayed at home when her husband was alive, and she certainly wasn't going to do so now that she was on her own. Four years later, as passionate as ever about the power of journalism to educate and inform, she founded *The Woman's Era.* She edited the stories, designed the pages, secured advertising, and did clerical work—a one-woman show, although not for long. Through her network she managed to secure national correspondents from as far away as Texas, California, and Colorado—including Elizabeth Piper Ensley, who reported on how suffrage was picking up steam in the western states.

Josephine did not mince words when it came to whom the paper was aimed at and what she hoped to achieve with its existence. Her main goal was to make sure that black women knew that they could do more than stay home and raise children. "Our indignation should know no limit," Josephine wrote in her paper. "We as women have been too unobtrusive, too little known."

In April 1900, she applied to attend the convention of the General Federation of Women's Clubs in Milwaukee. She was excited to go as a representative of the

Woman's Era Club. She would be the first-ever delegate from a black women's group, and the group would make history. There was just one small problem. When Josephine applied for the convention, she hadn't exactly mentioned the Woman's Era Club. She applied as a member of one of the two other clubs she belonged to—which were mostly white. But she believed that the federation should include everyone, so she packed her bags and got on the train.

With Josephine's light skin and straight hair, which she wore in a 1900s version of a topknot, it was fairly easy to confuse her with a

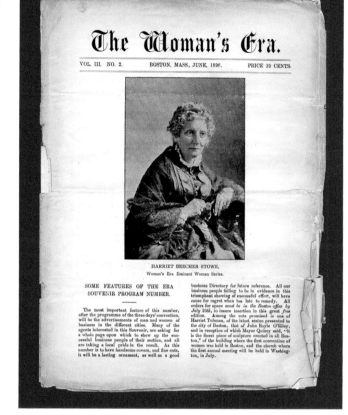

The June 1896 issue of The Woman's Era.

white woman. But as she was on her way from Boston to Milwaukee, two women who were also headed to the convention saw her waving hello to two black children on the train platform. The women were suspicious. Josephine, they realized, must be black, too.

When she arrived at the convention, the white women in charge confronted her. They refused to publicly acknowledge her as a delegate from the Woman's Era Club and demanded that she return her delegate badge. One woman even tried to rip it off Josephine's dress.

Josephine wouldn't back down. She had applied and been accepted, earning her place at the convention just like everyone else. And she wasn't going to hide who she was. She pulled herself away from the woman and left—with her badge.

When she got back to Boston, Josephine asked the Massachusetts State Federation of Women's Clubs, one of the oldest service organizations for women, for help. It formally asked the General Federation of Women's Clubs to allow the Woman's Era Club into its national organization. Newspapers and magazines from all over the country heard about the ordeal and reported on the debate. They called it "the Ruffin incident."

The General Federation of Women's Clubs had never accepted a club primarily composed of black women. And the white women in charge wanted to keep it that way. They attempted to save face by offering a "compromise." Fine, they said. Black women like Josephine could be delegates, but they could come only as representatives of mainly white clubs. That was not good enough for Josephine. She had spent her entire life fighting for equal, fair treatment for black women, and she wasn't going to settle for anything less.

Josephine had stopped publishing her paper by this point, but she lectured across the country about all the things she had learned in her life, and she helped

The offices of The Crisis, *the NAACP's magazine. W. E. B. Du Bois, one of the group's founders and the magazine's editor, is pictured top right. Circa 1910s.*

found Boston's chapter of the National Association for the Advancement of Colored People (NAACP). She continued to stand up for her rights and those of other black women.

She wrote about suffrage for the official NAACP magazine, *The Crisis,* and encouraged black men to support women's fight for the vote. "Many colored men doubt the wisdom of women suffrage because they fear that it will increase the number of our political enemies," she wrote in 1915. But she reassured readers that extending voting rights to women would not be an obstacle to racial equality. "The big women, the far seeing women, are in the ranks of the suffragists," she said. "We can afford to follow those women. We are justified in believing that the success of this movement for equality of the sexes means more progress toward equality of the races."

> "WE ARE JUSTIFIED IN BELIEVING THAT THE SUCCESS OF THIS MOVEMENT FOR EQUALITY OF THE SEXES **MEANS MORE PROGRESS TOWARD EQUALITY OF THE RACES.**"

Josephine died in 1924, four years after the Nineteenth Amendment was ratified. She was eighty-one years old. In 1999, the Massachusetts State House installed bronze busts of six women who were heroes of justice and equality, including the African American suffragists Sarah Parker Remond and Josephine St. Pierre Ruffin.

CHAPTER 5

Elizabeth Piper Ensley Goes West

IN THE 1800S, STATES AND TERRITORIES SUCH AS CALIFORNIA, COLORADO, Wyoming, and Utah were known as the Wild West because of their rugged terrain and sometimes hard living conditions. But the western United States was the region where women first won full voting rights in big numbers. The suffragists in that rough country traveled and campaigned widely. Even when the possibilities of winning the vote for women nationwide seemed dim, wins in the West gave women hope.

The first attempt to get women the vote came in 1854 in the Washington Territory and was defeated by just one vote. After the Civil War, momentum for suffrage began to grow. On December 10, 1869, the Wyoming Territory became the first to give women the right to vote. Next, on February 12, 1870, was the Utah Territory, where suffrage got support from the Mormon community, including Eliza Snow, the wife of the church leader Brigham Young. When Wyoming became a state in 1890, it insisted on keeping its provisions for women's rights—despite Congress's objections—and officially earned its place as the first of the United States where women could vote.

Elizabeth Piper Ensley moved into that world of possibility in the early 1890s. She had spent her twenties in Boston, where she became a schoolteacher, started a library, and got involved with civil rights and suffrage groups. She married Newell Ensley, a fellow teacher, and moved first to Washington, DC, where they both taught at Howard University, a historically black institution. After a short stint in Mississippi, they moved to Denver, where Elizabeth became the Denver reporter for Josephine St. Pierre Ruffin's newspaper, *The Woman's Era*. There was a lot to report on.

Putting up a billboard for the National Woman's Party. 1916.

Elizabeth cofounded the interracial group the Colorado Non-Partisan Equal Suffrage Association to make sure that black women were part of the growing suffrage movement in the West. Her efforts proved pivotal. In 1893, the association invited Carrie Chapman Catt to come to Colorado. Carrie, one of the leaders of the National American Woman Suffrage Association and one of the movement's most savvy strategists, later devised what she called the "Winning Plan," a blueprint to pass and ratify the Nineteenth Amendment.

Pro-suffrage postcard. 1910.

Carrie, who was white, spent weeks traveling across the state and campaigning for suffrage. The united front of black women and white women helped Colorado become, on November 7, 1893, the second state in the nation where women could vote.

The next year, when the women of Colorado went to the polls, Elizabeth described in *The Woman's Era* what it was like to see women standing in line to vote for the first time: "The clear atmosphere brought the mountains into bold relief. A glance at their strong outline, striking fearlessly against the cloudless sky, would fill any soul with inspiration. What wonder, then, that the women of Colorado stepped forth on the morning of the 6th of November, with enthusiasm unbounded, to exercise for the first time the crowning act of citizenship."

Colorado voters went on to elect the first three women to their state legislature in 1894. And in 1895, the *Boston Herald* reported, "Whatever may be thought of woman suffrage, the woman legislator appears to be a success in Colorado."

But still, not all women nationwide could vote, so Elizabeth Piper Ensley continued to work for universal suffrage. She also kept working to break down color barriers among organizers in Colorado, helping to integrate the Colorado Federation of Women's Clubs. She died in 1919, just a year before women won the vote nationwide. But she knew that the Nineteenth Amendment, while a critical milestone, was far from the end of the movement for equal rights. As she wrote, "Woman's work in politics must be like that of the chambered nautilus, the spiral animal, which after completing one house or shell proceeds to make another and so is constantly advancing."

"WOMAN'S WORK IN POLITICS MUST BE LIKE THAT OF THE CHAMBERED NAUTILUS, THE SPIRAL ANIMAL, WHICH AFTER COMPLETING ONE HOUSE OR SHELL PROCEEDS TO MAKE ANOTHER AND SO IS CONSTANTLY ADVANCING."

WILSON
IS
AGAINST
WOMEN
MR. PRESIDENT
THERE CAN ONLY BE NO NORMALCY
AMERICANS!
WHERE IS OUR FREE SPEECH
LIFTING
AS
WE CLIMB
VOTE
AGAINST WILS
HE OPPOSES
NATIONAL
WOMEN SUFF
MR. PRESIDEN
WE HAVE WAITED SIXT
ASKED BY YOU FOR RE
CASES OF POLITICAL
WE NOW DEMAND
THEIR IMMEDIATELY
SEEK
VOTES FROM WOMEN
WHEN HE OPPOSES
VOTES FROM WILSO
R LIBERT
PRESIDENT-
RICA FIRST?
LAST COUNTRY
WORLD TO
SE HER WARTIME
POLITICAL PRISONERS
MR. PRESIDENT
WHY BE DIFFER
ALL OTHER COUNTR
HAVE RELEASED T
POLITICAL PRISON
WHY NOT AMERICA?
VOTES
FOR
WOMEN

CHAPTER 6

Mary Church Terrell and the Power of Language

WHEN THE SENECA FALLS CONVENTION TOOK PLACE IN 1848 AND THOSE pioneering suffragists gathered, African American woman were not part of the conversation. Slavery was still the law of the land for more than three million black Americans in the South. For many of them, learning to read and write in English was illegal. Learning a foreign language seemed, for most, an impossible dream.

But sometimes freedom is a matter of timing. Mary Church Terrell knew that lesson well. She was born in Memphis, Tennessee, in September 1863—the middle of the Civil War. Her parents had been enslaved, but Mary was born free, and she charted a course of leadership that helped change the lives of women and men across the nation. She became a suffragist. She fought for the rights of all people of color. Holding America to the promises of the Founding Fathers—life, liberty, and the pursuit of happiness for all—became her life's work.

These dreams were supported early on by her parents, who were able to achieve success once they were free. Her father, Robert Church, was the son of an enslaved woman and a wealthy steamship owner who had allowed Robert to keep his wages, unlike most enslaved people. After Robert gained his freedom, he invested in real estate and became a wealthy man.

Mary wanted to study languages and travel the world, so she applied for and was accepted at Oberlin College, which was founded by abolitionists and was one of the first colleges in the United States to admit women and African Americans. There were very few black women at the school, but Mary found her classmates and teachers welcoming. She later wrote, "It would be difficult for a colored girl to go through a white school with fewer unpleasant experiences occasioned by race prejudice than I had." She wrote a paper there on the topic of suffrage, titled "Should an Amendment to the Constitution Allowing Women the Ballot Be Adopted?" Mary became one of the first black women to earn a college

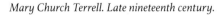

Mary Church Terrell. Late nineteenth century.

degree in the United States, graduating with a bachelor's in classics in 1884.

Later, after she completed a master's degree, Mary embarked on a two-year tour of Europe, traveling to France, Switzerland, Italy, and Germany and studying more languages. While there, she wrote in her diary in French or German, depending on which country she was in.

A National Association of Colored Women pin owned by Mary Church Terrell. Circa early twentieth century.

Mary had enjoyed some extraordinary privileges. During her first year at Oberlin, she was invited to Washington, DC, by Blanche K. Bruce, one of the first African American senators. He asked Mary to attend the inauguration of President James A. Garfield as his guest. It was during that trip that she met the great orator and activist Frederick Douglass. When she returned from Europe, she began to follow in his footsteps—using her gift for language to speak up for the causes she believed in.

While Mary traveled the world, the United States grew more unsteady. Lynching had become a form of domestic terrorism in the years after slavery. Over decades, thousands of black men and women were brutally killed by white mobs, and their murderers were never prosecuted. The government rarely made arrests in these cases, which only allowed the number of lynchings to grow. Mary and Frederick lobbied President Benjamin Harrison to publicly condemn lynching, but he never did. Still, Mary continued her work.

In 1895, Frederick died, and Mary became the first black woman appointed to the District of Columbia Board of Education. She later raised funds and visited schools, encouraging them to celebrate Douglass Day, a precursor to Black History Month, in his honor.

In 1896, the Supreme Court delivered its ruling in *Plessy v. Ferguson,* which

declared segregation permissible under the Constitution, as long as the segregated facilities and accommodations were "equal." But in reality, separate was rarely equal. That same year, Mary Church Terrell cofounded and became the first president of the National Association of Colored Women, a coalition of more than one hundred local black women's clubs. The organization's motto was "Lifting as we climb."

Around this time, Mary began to champion the cause of suffrage. She joined the National American Woman Suffrage Association (NAWSA) and was one of very few black members. Her years at Oberlin and abroad had made her comfortable in predominantly white groups, and she took NAWSA to task for excluding women of color, urging the 1898 convention to remember that suffrage for women of all colors was not just the "right thing to do." An inclusive movement, she reasoned, would grow in both power and perspective: "With courage, born of success achieved in the past, with a keen sense of the responsibility which we shall continue to assume, we look forward to a future large with promise and hope. Seeking no favors because of our color, nor patronage because of our needs, we knock at the bar of justice, asking an equal chance."

> "SEEKING NO FAVORS BECAUSE OF OUR COLOR, NOR PATRONAGE BECAUSE OF OUR NEEDS, WE KNOCK AT THE BAR OF JUSTICE, ASKING AN EQUAL CHANCE."

In 1904, Mary was invited to speak at the International Congress of Women in Berlin, Germany. The cost to attend the congress was considerable, and Mary and her husband, Robert, whom she had married in 1891, were comfortable, but not rich. She was a school board member. He was a judge. But her husband encouraged her to go, despite the expense. Once again, she was the only black woman

in attendance. She delivered her speech to the congress in Berlin on June 13, 1904. She used her background and knowledge as a linguist and teacher to give her speech, titled "The Progress of Colored Women," three times—in German, French, and English.

Mary Church Terrell, at left, with a fur stole, and Mary McLeod Bethune, at right, with a white brooch. Circa 1947.

She began by reminding her audience that her parents had been enslaved, that her very being was a testament to how far one could travel on the road to freedom in a single lifetime. "If anyone had had the courage to predict fifty years ago that a woman with African blood in her veins would journey from the United States to Berlin, Germany, to address an International Congress of Women in the year 1904," she told the audience, "he would either have been laughed to scorn or he would have been immediately confined in an asylum for the hopelessly insane."

Mary knew that freedom for all was never about one battle. No single great win—the abolition of slavery, the passage of the Nineteenth Amendment—would right the wrongs in a country founded on such injustices as slavery and the denial of women's rights. But perhaps what made her life most extraordinary is how much joy she got from each small victory, how much stamina she displayed in her decades-long career as an activist. In 1953, the year before Mary died, her hometown paper *The Washington Post* wrote: "There have been many battles and many victories in Mrs. Terrell's long and energetic life. . . . It may fairly be said of her that when she fought bigotry it was never with hatred; she met lethargy and prejudice with spirit and understanding. And she won the hearts as well as the minds of men."

hat surprised when you find out who the writ
this letter is.
have been intend
g to write a
you before thi
erhaps you wil
iting to you th
easy to expla
you for ha
g acted so
were visitin
Washington
I heard th
u had lef
rget how
ave treated
ought yo
ould cast a
to that de
asm kno
t from th
ges of yo
aid to yo
ngelina
e Friend.
n in Mr.
in scho
think qui
ten how
sed to com
ou at tend
at dear
I have spe
many
her Mr. E.
Brown sends
tle pupil." (
e says.) Could
once more, in t
d sweet way, just
at your calling, and like a
ngel bending o'er you breathe into your ear, "I love you

Angelina Weld Grimké, Mary Burrill, and the Queer Leaders of the Suffrage Movement

"OH MAMIE, IF YOU ONLY KNEW HOW MY HEART BEATS WHEN I THINK OF YOU. . . . I know you are too young now to become my wife, but I hope, darling, that in a few years you will come to me and be my love, my wife!"

These passionate words were penned in 1896 by Angelina Weld Grimké, a sixteen-year-old girl who grew up to become a suffragist and a poet. The words "lesbian" and "gay" weren't really used at the time. But that doesn't mean that women who loved other women did not exist. Angelina formed romantic connections with several young women, including Mary Karn—the Mamie in this letter—and Mary Burrill, a future playwright and, like Angelina, a suffragist.

Angelina and Mary Burrill were part of a community of black women, which included Mary Church Terrell, living in Washington, DC, at the turn of the century. They were super smart, well-educated, and passionate about equality and voting rights. But they weren't fighting only for the right to vote: they also believed that women should be able to make choices about all aspects of their lives, such as where to live and what to study and which careers to pursue—and whom to spend their lives with.

These women refused to fit into traditional molds of what a lady should be. "It isn't simply a case of who's gay and who's not," the historian Susan Ware writes in *Why They Marched: Untold Stories of the Women Who Fought for the Right to Vote.* "To speak of 'queering the suffrage movement' is to identify it as a space where women felt free to express a wide range of gender nonconforming behaviors." The suffragists had found their voices, and they weren't about to go back to being quiet and polite and letting men tell them what to do—even after they got the vote. As Angelina put it, "When women become equal with men, the injustices will end."

Suffrage history is full of clues suggesting that queer relationships existed in all ranks of the movement. Terms such as "Boston marriage"—referring to two financially independent women who set up house together and lived as partners—often alluded to deep friendships that may well have been romantic relationships.

Mary Burrill spent much of her adult life in one such relationship, with Lucy Diggs Slowe,

Angelina Weld Grimké. 1923.

who was the first dean of women at Howard University. The women shared an off-campus house on Kearny Street for some fifteen years, hosting parties and salons for their suffragist friends and for female students at Howard. The school tried to make Lucy leave her home—and Mary—and live on campus. But Lucy refused to leave.

> **"TO SPEAK OF 'QUEERING THE SUFFRAGE MOVEMENT' IS TO IDENTIFY IT AS A SPACE WHERE WOMEN FELT FREE TO EXPRESS A WIDE RANGE OF GENDER NON-CONFORMING BEHAVIORS."**

When Lucy died, in 1937, it was Mary who made the funeral arrangements, accepted people's condolences, and wrote her beloved partner's eulogy. "I, who have known her as a girl and woman for 35 years, as her teacher, her colleague, and her friend, am happy and honored to perform this simple task," Mary wrote of Lucy, "for it is a duty of mingled joy and pain, tempered by a great admiration and a warm personal affection."

The suffrage movement—and women's history in general—is full of examples like Mary and Lucy, who found ways to be together even at a time when their love was not accepted by society. In fact, although the history books don't usually talk about this part of their lives, some of the most prominent leaders of the suffrage movement were part of what we would now call the lesbian, gay, bisexual, transgender, and/or queer (LGBTQ) community.

In Pennsylvania, Lucy Anthony, the niece of

Lucy Diggs Slowe, seated at right, and Mary Burrill at their home in Washington, DC. Circa 1920s.

Susan B. Anthony (who herself never married and is widely believed to have had romantic relationships with women), spent much of her life with Dr. Anna Howard Shaw, a physician and Methodist minister known for her powerful public speaking. Anna served as president of the National American Woman Suffrage Association (NAWSA)—which was cofounded by none other than Susan—and she was one of the most prominent voices speaking about suffrage in the early 1900s. She also found ways to express her identity that weren't in line with traditional ideas of nineteenth-century womanhood. Outspoken and opinionated, she wore her hair short, and even as a kid she preferred to work outside with the boys rather than stay inside learning household skills with her mom. She loved going out into the forest and standing on a stump, talking to the trees to practice preaching.

In New York, there was Carrie Chapman Catt, the woman who worked with Elizabeth Piper Ensley to help Colorado achieve suffrage. Carrie started out as a teacher after graduating from what is now Iowa State University—the only woman in her class. She joined the Iowa Woman Suffrage Association in the late 1880s and then became involved with NAWSA, eventually taking over as president when Susan B. Anthony stepped down in 1900. She left the organization briefly in 1904 (when Anna took over), but returned as president again in 1915, serving until 1920 and spearheading the "Winning Plan" to pass the Nineteenth Amendment.

Carrie was married twice—first to a newspaper editor named Leo Chapman, who died of typhoid the year after their wedding, and then to an engineer named George Catt. George and Carrie had an arrangement: while he stayed at home, she traveled the country for months at a time, organizing and campaigning for the vote. Around the same time that she married George, Carrie met Mary Garrett Hay, another suffragist, whom she called Mollie Brown Eyes. It was love at first sight, and Mollie soon began accompanying Carrie on her travels.

When George died, Carrie and Mollie moved in together. In 1919, they bought an estate in upstate New York, called Juniper Ledge, which became a monument to their work.

Carrie and Mollie spent several happy years together at Juniper Ledge. Carrie stayed involved in the fight for women's rights, writing a history of the suffrage movement and founding the League of Women Voters to help educate women about how to exercise their new right to the ballot. But she loved escaping to the countryside and relaxing with her partner. The pair would spend long evenings kicking back in the estate's twenty-room mansion.

Mollie died in 1928. When Carrie followed, nineteen years later, she insisted that she be buried with Mollie. Her wish was honored, and the women now rest together forever in Woodlawn Cemetery in New York. The inscription on their monument is a testament to their relationship.

"Here lie two," it says, "united in friendship for thirty-eight years through constant service to a great cause."

Carrie Chapman Catt, at left, and Mary Garrett Hay voting. November 1918.

SUIT YOURSELF

The suffrage movement was full of women like Angelina Weld Grimké and Carrie Chapman Catt, who bucked tradition. Another one of those women was Dr. Mary Walker.

Mary was born in 1832 in Oswego, New York. Her parents believed in raising their children to think freely and to question traditions that didn't sit well with them. They wanted their daughters to be as well educated as their son, so they started a school in their town. And their marriage didn't operate according to the gender norms of the day. Mary's mother often did hard physical labor on the farm, and her father did daily household tasks.

Mary graduated from Syracuse Medical College in 1855. She married a fellow medical student, Albert Miller, and they opened a practice together. She later served as an assistant surgeon during the Civil War—at which time she wore a military uniform, just like the men—and she was captured by Confederate troops who held her prisoner for four months. She would eventually become the only woman in American history to be awarded the Medal of Honor.

Dr. Mary Walker wearing her Medal of Honor. Circa 1866.

As a doctor, and as a girl who'd grown up on a farm, Mary believed deeply that she should be free to be comfortable, to wear what she wanted, and she felt that all women should be allowed to do the same. By the 1870s, she regularly wore trousers, a vest, a coat, and a top hat. Even women in the suffrage movement had a hard time supporting the way she dressed. And she was arrested—repeatedly—for wearing men's clothing.

After the war, Mary campaigned actively for health care, women's rights, and dress reform. She was a member of the Central Women's Suffrage Bureau in Washington, DC, and while there, she raised funds to endow a female chair at Howard University. She declared herself a candidate for the Senate in 1881 and for Congress in 1890. She didn't win either election, but she did testify before Congress about the importance of suffrage.

Mary died in 1919, just one year before the Nineteenth Amendment was ratified. To the end, she rejected the idea that she dressed like a man. She wore what was comfortable and what suited her lifestyle. She would say, "I don't wear men's clothes, I wear my own clothes." Always a woman who thought for herself, Mary decided that when she died, she wanted to be buried in a suit—*her* suit. And so she was.

Dr. Mary Walker in her trousers and coat, with her Medal of Honor on her lapel. Circa 1870.

CHAPTER 8

Mabel Ping-Hua Lee's Great Parade

When Mabel Ping-Hua Lee moved to New York City as a child around 1905, there were relatively few Chinese immigrants on the East Coast. In 1910, the census reported that there were 5,266 people of Chinese descent living in the city, many of them in "Chinatown" in lower Manhattan. It was a new community, and the streets were alive with delicious smells, bright colors, and voices from halfway around the world.

By 1912, Mabel and her parents were living on Bayard Street in Chinatown, and they had made a name for themselves. Mabel's father was a minister whose fluency in English allowed him to help the community engage with the rest of the

city. He led the First Chinese Baptist Church and was so active in the community that some referred to him as the neighborhood's unofficial mayor.

Everyone also knew the daughter of the "mayor," and they knew how smart she was. At the time, not everyone believed that girls needed to go to college, but everyone in the community knew that none of this old thinking applied to Mabel. She attended Erasmus Hall High School in Brooklyn and had big plans to attend the women's-only Barnard College, the sister school to the then all-male Columbia College. She hoped to return to China one day to open a school for girls. She felt lucky to have the opportunity to study in the United States, but she wanted young girls in China to have good opportunities back home as well.

Still, there was a limit to how much the community would stand behind her. And Mabel crossed the line when she got involved with the suffrage movement. The suffragists were considered radical—how dare they fight so steadfastly for equal rights?—but Mabel believed that voting was the key that would open every important door for women. Women's rights were a big issue in China, too, and Mabel wanted to be part of the movement in the United States—even though she knew that, if the Nineteenth Amendment passed, she herself would be unable to vote, because the US Chinese Exclusion Act of 1882 had severely limited

Mabel Ping-Hua Lee. Circa 1920s.

immigration from China and prevented those who came to the United States from becoming citizens.

Still, she joined the cause and convinced her mother to join, too.

Her mother's participation in suffrage was so controversial that newspapers—such as *The New York Tribune*—even wrote about it: "Tongues are still wagging in Chinatown over the fact that Mrs. Lee . . . went to a suffrage meeting. Mabel Lee, her daughter, is, of course, a hopeless little suffragette, who has already promised to march in the parade."

In 1912, Mabel, who was just sixteen, led a contingent of Chinese and Chinese American women in one of the biggest suffrage parades in US history. *The New York Times* reported, "Ten thousand strong, the army of those who believe in the cause of woman's suffrage marched up Fifth Avenue at sundown yesterday in a parade the like of which New York never knew before."

Mabel didn't merely march: she rode a white horse at the start of the parade, and she wore a three-cornered hat in the colors of the British suffrage movement: purple to symbolize that the cause of suffrage was noble; white for purity; and green, the color of spring, as a symbol of hope. (American suffragists usually substituted the gold of the sunflowers of Kansas—where they waged some of their earliest campaigns—for green.)

Excerpt from The New York Times's *coverage of the 1912 suffrage march in New York.*

A sash in the traditional colors of the American suffrage movement. 1920.

In the fall, Mabel began her studies at Barnard College. She majored in history and philosophy, wrote articles about suffrage and feminism for *The Chinese Students' Monthly,* and gave a speech, "The Submerged Half," which encouraged the Chinese immigrant community to promote girls' education and women's rights. In it, she said: "The welfare of China and possibly its very existence as an independent nation depend on rendering tardy justice to its womankind. For no nation can ever make real and lasting progress in civilization unless its women are following close to its men if not actually abreast with them."

> "NO NATION CAN EVER MAKE REAL AND LASTING PROGRESS IN CIVILIZATION UNLESS ITS WOMEN ARE FOLLOWING CLOSE TO ITS MEN IF NOT ACTUALLY ABREAST WITH THEM."

Charlotte Brooks, the author of *American Exodus: Second-Generation Chinese Americans in China, 1901–1949,* explains: "Something a lot of people in the US don't realize is that Mabel's activism grew out of China's New Culture Movement, which included the idea that the suppression of women, and the poor treatment of women, were both holding China back and represented a kind of backwardness. A lot of the Chinese students who were with her at Columbia were influenced by this movement. Then, after they graduated and returned to China, they encountered the May Fourth Movement, which was the moment the modern Chinese nation was born. She was part of this particular generation. She was part of this transpacific conversation both figuratively and literally, since she went back and forth to China as well."

Mabel went on to get a PhD in economics from Columbia University, becoming the first Chinese woman to earn a doctorate degree there. In 1921, she published *The Economic History of China: With Special Reference to Agriculture.*

Although women's suffrage became law in 1920, it wasn't until 1943, when the Chinese Exclusion Act was repealed, that Mabel and other Chinese immigrant suffragists were finally granted the rights they had fought so hard to achieve.

Mabel eventually took over as the director of her father's church, and she founded the Chinese Christian Center, a community center on Pell Street that offered English classes, health services, a kindergarten, and job training to people in New York's Chinese community. She became an example of what a woman can do when given the chance to learn and lead. As she wrote of China, "In the fierce struggle for existence among the nations, that nation is badly handicapped which leaves undeveloped one half of its intellectual and moral resources." The same, of course, was true of the United States.

Mabel Ping-Hua Lee with kindergarten students at the Chinese Christian Center in New York. 1941.

CHAPTER 9

Ida B. Wells-Barnett

Marching Forward

THE DATE WAS MARCH 3, 1913. FROM ALL AROUND THE COUNTRY, WOMEN flocked to Washington, DC, for the biggest parade the nation's capital had ever seen: the Woman Suffrage Procession. Hundreds of women, organized by Alice Paul, Lucy Burns, and the National American Woman Suffrage Association (NAWSA), spilled out of train cars. Hundreds more hiked two hundred miles from New York. They came with hope, with determination, with a plan to make their demands known in the nation's capital. The proposition: women should have the same rights as men, including the right to vote.

The protest was scheduled just before another major event—Woodrow

Cover of the official program for the National American Woman Suffrage Association march in Washington, DC. 1913.

Wilson's inauguration as president (back then, presidents weren't sworn in until March)—but as it turned out, more people came to see the suffrage parade than came to see the president. About eight thousand people—women and men—would march in it, and five hundred thousand more would come to watch. The energy in the air was electrifying.

Ida B. Wells-Barnett had come all the way from Chicago with her friends—two white women named Belle Squire and Virginia Brooks, who were also part of the Illinois delegation. But the leadership of the parade was concerned that the white suffragists who had come from the South would not be welcoming toward black women and might refuse to march alongside them, thus diminishing the parade's numbers. Ida was told that she would have to move to the back.

Ida fumed. She knew that some white women in the suffrage movement thought of black women as inferior because of the color of their skin. It was time for this to change, and the leadership of the parade had the power to make it happen. Shouldn't they be happy that there were African American protesters joining the cause and making the numbers stronger overall? Why couldn't they see the bigger picture?

Ida decided that she wasn't going down without a fight.

"If the Illinois women do not take a stand now in this great democratic parade, then the colored women are lost," she protested.

Grace Trout, who was leading the Illinois delegation, was moved. She invited Ida to march with them, but when she went to tell the rest of the leadership, they stood firm in their decision to send Ida to the back of the parade. Ida walked away in disgust.

But she had a plan.

When the parade started, rather than go to the back, Ida stood on the sidelines with the spectators, waiting. When the Illinois delegation marched by, she spotted her friends, Belle and Virginia, jumped in, and walked with them throughout the rest of the march.

Ida B. Wells-Barnett. Circa 1893.

Ida was born into slavery in Holly Springs, Mississippi, in 1862, the eldest of James and Elizabeth (Warrenton) Wells's eight children. She was a child when slavery was abolished in 1865, and her mother became known in the community as a famous cook. Her father thrived in the years after emancipation, becoming a successful carpenter and a trustee of the historically black Rust College. He became involved in community activism and was well known as a "race man"—an activist dedicated to racial justice.

When Ida was sixteen, her parents died from yellow fever within twenty-four hours of each other. Her younger brother also became sick and died. Suddenly she found herself alone, having to support her six younger siblings. She dropped out of school and got a job as a teacher, first at a rural school outside Holly Springs and then at one in Tennessee that offered better pay. The conditions there for black citizens were terrible. Slavery had been abolished, but the federal government, ceding control to individual states, had backed out of many laws originally meant to protect African Americans.

Ida was subject to these conditions as much as anyone, but she was a fighter, and this time she pushed back with her pen. She became a journalist, writing articles about racial inequality for a newspaper called *The Memphis Free Speech and Headlight,* which later shortened its name to *The Memphis Free Speech.*

In March 1892, Ida's friend Thomas Moss was violently attacked and killed, along with two other black men—Calvin McDowell and Will Stewart. Thomas ran a successful store in Memphis called People's Grocery, where Calvin and Will worked. When racial tensions in the area escalated that spring, a string of violent incidents erupted. White police officers rounded up dozens of black men from the neighborhood—including Thomas and his employees—and arrested them. One night, a large group of white men stormed the jail. They dragged Thomas, Calvin, and Will out and took them to a railroad yard outside the city, where they brutally beat and shot them.

Ida was horrified.

She wrote a series of angry articles about the injustices of racial violence and started a campaign against lynching, carefully recording attacks across the region so people would know what was going on. In 1892, she published *Southern Horrors,* her landmark book about lynching. She said, "The way to right wrongs is to turn the light of truth upon them."

Her stories got a lot of attention—good and bad—and she began receiving death threats. One day, a white mob stormed the newspaper offices and trashed the place. Ida wasn't there at the time, but she was frightened, and smart enough to flee, eventually settling in Chicago.

> ## "THE WAY TO RIGHT WRONGS IS TO TURN THE LIGHT OF TRUTH UPON THEM."

As a northern city without Jim Crow laws, Chicago was safer. Ida started a new life there, where she married Ferdinand Barnett, a lawyer and an activist. They had four children.

Ida saw suffrage as an extension of her work against the horrors of lynching. It helped that she had a supportive husband who believed in her.

She knew that the only way the situation for African Americans could improve was for the laws to change. They needed an African American person to win public office and fight for them, and for that to happen, more African Americans needed to vote. This could be accomplished if women could vote, too.

To that end, she helped start the National Negro Committee, which would

Pro-suffrage protest in Chicago. 1916.

eventually become the National Association for the Advancement of Colored People (NAACP). But giving black women a voice—and a space—of their own was always on Ida's mind.

In January 1913, she found true allies in Belle Squire and Virginia Brooks—the white friends she would join during the women's march in Washington later that year. With their support, she started the Alpha Suffrage Club for black women in Chicago.

Women in Illinois got the right to vote in local and presidential races (although not yet on the state level) in 1913. The Alpha Suffrage Club quickly grew to about two hundred members. The group started a newsletter and canvassed neighborhoods to encourage people to vote for African American candidates.

In 1915, Oscar De Priest became Chicago's first African American alderman. About one thousand black women went to the polls, showing how powerful they could be as a force. After suffrage was won in 1920, Oscar became the first African American from Illinois elected to the US Congress—in part because of all the women who supported him. (Almost one hundred years later, another African American lawmaker from Chicago, named Barack Obama, would make history by becoming the first black president of the United States.)

Ida would spend the rest of her life fighting injustices, and as Chicago grew to be a vibrant city, she made it known that black Americans must have a fair place in it.

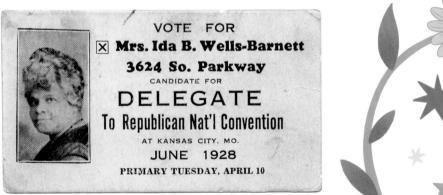

VOTE FOR
☒ **Mrs. Ida B. Wells-Barnett**
3624 So. Parkway
CANDIDATE FOR
DELEGATE
To Republican Nat'l Convention
AT KANSAS CITY. MO.
JUNE 1928
PRIMARY TUESDAY, APRIL 10

Candidate card supporting Ida B. Wells-Barnett as a delegate
to the Republican National Convention. 1928.

FROM MOVEMENT TO REVOLUTION

By the early 1900s, women had been fighting for the right to vote for more than half a century. They had held meetings, such as the Seneca Falls Convention, to exchange ideas. Eloquent speakers such as Frances Ellen Watkins Harper had laid out their case for the vote. And they had staged peaceful protests. But despite all these efforts, they were still unable to vote in the vast majority of the United States.

Meanwhile, the women of Britain had been fighting a parallel battle for the vote. They had used many of the same tactics as the Americans—petitions, speeches, meetings—but that was about to change.

In October 1903, a woman named Emmeline Pankhurst, fed up with the lack of progress in British women's fight for the vote, helped form the Women's Social and Political Union (WSPU). Their motto was "Deeds not words."

"There is something that governments care for far more than human life, and that is the security of property," Emmeline told her fellow organizers in a 1912 speech. "And so it is through property that we shall strike the enemy." It wasn't enough just to keep talking about the vote: they had to make those in power listen. "Be militant each in your own way," she instructed the members of the WSPU, who called themselves suffragettes—embracing a term coined by a *Daily Mail* journalist to disparage them and using it to signify their dedication to radical action.

Aftermath of a suffragette arson attack on Saunderton Station in Buckinghamshire, England. 1913.

The suffragette Annie Kenney being arrested during a demonstration in London. Circa 1913.

Emmeline concluded her speech, "I incite this meeting to rebellion."

The suffragettes didn't wholly abandon their old strategies—they continued to organize marches and petitions and give powerful speeches about the need for the vote—but they also broke windows, planted bombs, and took other militant action. They were arrested repeatedly and beaten by police. But they refused to back down.

This radical shift inspired some American women's rights advocates, who had begun to wonder whether, after more than fifty years of activism, suffrage would ever come to pass. As Josephine St. Pierre Ruffin had written about Jim Crow laws in *The Woman's Era,* "If laws are unjust, they must be continually broken until they are killed or altered." American women were no longer satisfied with petitions and pamphlets. They were ready to break some rules, if not the actual law.

One of those women was Alice Paul. In 1907, the future leader of the 1913 Woman Suffrage Procession in Washington—in which Ida B. Wells-Barnett would walk—moved to England. She joined the suffragettes at their protests and was arrested several times. She even served one month's hard labor as punishment and was force-fed when she went on a hunger strike. She also met an American student named Lucy Burns, who had left Oxford to join the suffragette fight. (The women actually met in a London police station while under arrest for participating in a WSPU protest.) They became fast friends, and partners in the fight for the vote.

When Alice and Lucy returned to the United States, they brought the spirit, and the impatience, of the suffragettes with them. It was time, they believed, for American women to embrace the words of Emmeline Pankhurst. "Men make the moral code and they expect women to accept it. They have decided that it is entirely right and proper for men to fight for their liberties and their rights, but that it is not right and proper for women to fight for theirs," Emmeline had written. But women had let men make all the decisions for far too long. It was time for the suffrage fight to go from a movement to a revolution.

> "MEN MAKE THE MORAL CODE AND THEY EXPECT WOMEN TO ACCEPT IT. THEY HAVE DECIDED THAT IT IS ENTIRELY RIGHT AND PROPER FOR MEN TO FIGHT FOR THEIR LIBERTIES AND THEIR RIGHTS, BUT THAT IT IS NOT RIGHT AND PROPER FOR WOMEN TO FIGHT FOR THEIRS."

Alice and Lucy joined the Congressional Committee of the National American Woman Suffrage Association (NAWSA) in 1912. While they did not embrace the WSPU's violent tactics, they did encourage their fellow activists to take to the streets, favoring marches and protests over petitions and speeches. This created a rift in NAWSA, and they eventually split with such old-school suffragists as Carrie Chapman Catt, who took a more traditional approach. Alice and Lucy formed their own, action-focused group, which would eventually become the National Woman's Party (NWP).

The NWP made protests a cornerstone of their strategy. Members of the party picketed the White House, a bold move that had never been done before. These women were called the Silent Sentinels because they did not speak, letting their signs do the talking instead. Mary Church Terrell and her daughter sometimes joined the Sentinels, even though the dangers of being arrested were particularly great for them as African American women.

Many of the Silent Sentinel signs addressed the president directly, with pleas such as

Mr. President, How Long Must Women Wait for Liberty?

and

Mr. President, What Will You Do for Woman Suffrage?

As *The Washington Post* reported in 1917, the Sentinels aimed for it to be "impossible for the President to enter or leave the White House without encountering a sentinel bearing some device pleading the suffrage cause."

Silent Sentinels protesting in front of the White House. Circa 1917.

Crowds gathered to heckle the Sentinels. Some anti-suffrage protesters threw eggs and tomatoes at the women. As in Britain, the demonstrators were treated roughly by the police. Many of them were imprisoned. In jail, they were forced to sleep on narrow cots infested with bedbugs and eat maggot-ridden food. Some were beaten by guards, and some went on hunger strikes and were violently force-fed. Alice Paul was even sent to a psychiatric ward. But these efforts did not always help the anti-suffrage cause: on the contrary, the media coverage of the suffragists' plight sometimes created sympathy for their movement.

The NWP also helped bring together women from different walks of life in the suffrage fight. Alva Vanderbilt Belmont, an extremely wealthy white woman, became one of the NWP's leaders and helped integrate the suffrage movement. She invited African American women and immigrant women to weekend retreats at Beacon Towers, her mansion on the North Shore of Long Island, and was a dedicated supporter of working women's rights, organizing marches to support striking factory workers and raising funds to cover their missed wages. She also set up "suffrage settlement houses" around New York City and on Long Island, where women could gather, take classes, and learn about the fight for the vote. When one of these

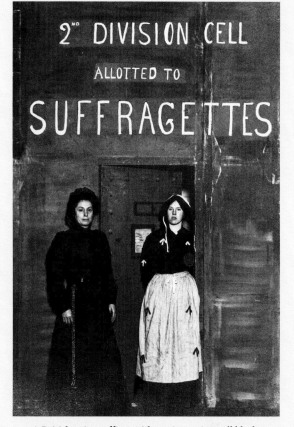

A British prison officer with a prisoner in a cell block designated for suffragettes. Circa 1910.

houses debuted in Harlem in 1910, *The New York Times* reported that Alva told the large opening night crowd, "This house is here to ask you to help spread the knowledge of the woman suffrage movement, first in the home, then in the city, and then in the State." The headline on the story read "Harlem Women Organize."

Together, these actions—both peaceful and radical, across races and classes—brought American suffrage closer to being a reality.

CHAPTER 10

Jovita Idár

El voto para las mujeres

THE POLICE OFFICERS IN LAREDO, TEXAS, WEREN'T HAPPY. THE NEWSPAPER *El Progreso* had just run an editorial that angered a lot of people: it criticized President Woodrow Wilson for his decision to send US troops to occupy the Mexican city of Veracruz. The year was 1914, and just across the border from Texas, the Mexican Revolution was raging.

People in Mexico were angry with their dictator, President Porfirio Díaz, because he made sure that wealth and power belonged only to a select few. People were tired of not having any money and not being allowed to express their opinions. Injustice was everywhere.

Texas had been part of Mexico until 1836, when it declared independence. But, even after it was annexed by the United States nine years later, people often traveled back and forth across the border easily. After the Revolution broke out, in 1910, Mexican people began fleeing to Texas to escape the violence. But once they arrived, they faced intense racism from white Texans. Tensions were high when *El Progreso*'s editorial came out.

The police officers, who were part of the Texas Ranger force, pulled up to the newspaper's offices with a plan: they were going to shut the paper down. But as they prepared to storm the entrance, they found a woman blocking the doorway.

Jovita Idár, an educated woman who always took care to dress well, was highly respected in the community—not somebody who could simply be pushed aside. The Rangers retreated, but they returned the next day, when Jovita wasn't there,

Jovita Idár, second from the right, in the print shop of El Progreso *in Laredo, Texas. Circa 1914.*

and proceeded to sack the building, badly beat one of the paper's employees, and destroy the printing press.

That didn't stop Jovita. She and her brothers started another newspaper, called *Evolución*. In a letter, she proudly told a friend that she had even bought the new printing press herself.

Jovita wrote many of *Evolución*'s articles, as she had at *El Progreso*. Over the years, she argued for better schools, more economic opportunities, and fairer treatment for Mexican Americans—and for women's rights, including the right to vote.

She wrote in one article: "Working women . . . proudly raise your chins and face the fight. The time of your degradation has passed!"

> "WORKING WOMEN . . . PROUDLY RAISE YOUR CHINS AND FACE THE FIGHT. THE TIME OF YOUR DEGRADATION HAS PASSED!"

You won't find Jovita in many history books, partly because historians are still trying to piece together the stories of her and other Latina activists, whose letters and other papers were not always saved. But her life shows just how important these women were in the push for equal rights—and just how complicated the question of equal rights could be for Latinas.

Jovita was born in 1885 in Laredo. The Idár family, of which Jovita was one of eight children, had a comfortable middle-class life—when Jovita was a teenager, her father, Nicasio, became the publisher of a newspaper called *La Crónica*—but Texas was hardly an easy place for people of Mexican origin.

Shop windows sometimes had signs telling them to keep out. Mexican children were taught in segregated schools, with fewer supplies and less qualified teachers. Mexican men were sometimes lynched.

Jovita originally worked as a teacher, but she grew frustrated with the unequal conditions for Mexican children, so in 1910 she joined the staff of her father's newspaper, where she could fight for change.

The Idárs weren't just journalists: they were also activists. In 1911, they helped organize El Primer Congreso Mexicanista (the First Mexicanist Congress), a meeting of activists concerned with issues facing the community. As part of the congress, Jovita also helped found the League of Mexican Women, which may have been the first Mexican American feminist organization.

That same year, Jovita—who sometimes wrote under the pen name Astrea, for the Greek goddess of justice—published an article in favor of women's suffrage. And she wasn't the only Latina in the United States arguing for the right to vote.

Some Latina suffragists worked alongside white women in big national organizations. In New Mexico, Adelina Otero-Warren led the fight to get her state's legislators to approve the Nineteenth Amendment. (She also became the first Latina to run for the US Congress, in 1922.)

Others were more radical, like Luisa Capetillo, a Puerto Rican labor leader, who fought for workers' rights in Puerto Rico and up and down the East Coast, from New York to Florida. Like Dr. Mary Walker, she thought that women should dress the way

Adelina Otero-Warren. 1923.

they wanted: sometimes she wore men's clothes, including a tie and vest, while organizing. In Cuba, her clothes once got her arrested, on the grounds that they were disturbing the peace!

The rights of Latinas, like the rights of all women, depended a lot on the laws and customs of the state where they lived. And in Texas, voting rights were much more complicated for Latinas and other women of color than for their white sisters. So the Nineteenth Amendment didn't necessarily mean that women like Jovita could vote.

Under the US Constitution, many decisions about who can vote are left up to the states. For a long time, you didn't have to be an American citizen to vote in elections in many states, including Texas. But in the early twentieth century, anti-immigrant sentiment was rising across the country, and laws changed so that only Americans citizens could vote. In Texas, this meant that many Texans who had been born on the Mexican side of the border, or in other places outside the United States, actually *lost* the right to vote.

There were some white suffragists who worked to make sure that their Latina and African American sisters would also get the vote. But for many, the important thing was that *they* got the equal rights that had long been denied them, and they saw immigrants, including Mexicans, as standing in their way.

Many white women, like white men, owing to their own racist and anti-immigrant views, opposed noncitizens voting. But some suffragists also feared that immigrant men might have more traditional views about the family and would vote against women's suffrage.

Texas did begin allowing women to vote in primary elections in 1918, two years before the Nineteenth Amendment was ratified. But that *still* didn't mean all citizens could always vote.

In 1923, Texas passed a law creating what is called a "white primary"—

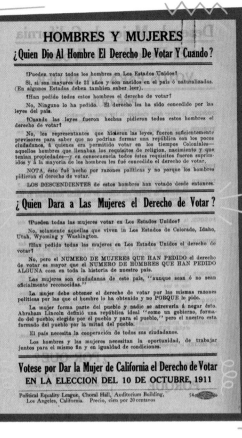

Pro-suffrage poster from California. 1911.

meaning that only white voters could choose a party's candidate. Under this system, black women and men were legally barred from voting in the Democratic primary .

For Mexican Americans, it was more complicated. Under the law, they were technically considered white. But they were often kept away from the polls by literacy tests, poll taxes, and other exclusionary practices.

Some people challenged this system, including the Idárs. In 1929, Jovita's brother Eduardo helped start a group called the League of United Latin American Citizens (LULAC). It fought for voting rights as well as better schools and broader civil rights for Latinos. In the early days, LULAC was for men. They started allowing women to join in 1932—but only in separate, all-female chapters.

But even before that, Jovita was in the fight. In the period after the Nineteenth Amendment was ratified, she was active in the Democratic Party. She even worked as a precinct judge—in other words, she became one of the people running the elections.

Jovita died in 1946, but the women who followed in her footsteps have continued to push against barriers to fight for equal rights. Vilma Martínez, who was a college student in Texas in the 1960s, was told not to get her hopes up about law school. "I went anyway," she recalled in an interview for this book.

In law school, she was told not to get her hopes up about becoming a litigator, the kind of lawyer who helps people bring lawsuits to court. (Even today, litigators are largely men.) She became one anyway, and at the age of twenty-nine became the president of the Mexican American Legal Defense and Educational Fund (MALDEF) in Washington, DC.

In 1965, the landmark Voting Rights Act ended the legal discrimination against African Americans at the polls. In 1975, MALDEF led the effort to convince Congress to pass a law extending its protections to Mexican Americans and other minority groups.

One of the most important parts of the new law was a rule allowing many citizens whose first language wasn't English to have access to voting materials in their language. After all, how can you vote if you can't read the ballot?

Vilma, who later became the US ambassador to Argentina, said that helping to pass that law was one of her proudest accomplishments. And she added that it is important to learn more about Latinas like Jovita who fought for equal rights.

"The right to vote was so hard-fought," she said. "We need to value it and exercise it."

The VOTES for WOMEN Game

START HERE

JUNE 4, 1919 PASSES SENATE

✳ You get all your neighbors to sign a petition in favor of the Nineteenth Amendment! **Move ahead 2 spaces.**

JUNE 10 Wisconsin, Illinois & Michigan

NOVEMBER 5 Maine

JANUARY 6, 1920 Kentucky & Rhode Island

JANUARY 13 Oregon

NOVEMBER 1 California

✳ A suffrage cartoon you drew is published in a prominent newspaper! **Move ahead 3 spaces.**

FEBRUARY 11 Idaho

✗ Your state's senator gives a speech at an anti-suffrage rally. **Go back 2 spaces.** ✗

DECEMBER 1 North Dakota

✗ Your aunt and uncle storm out of Christmas dinner when you bring up the progress toward ratification. **Go back 5 spaces.** ✗

FEBRUARY 9 New Jersey

JANUARY 16 Indiana

SEPTEMBER 30 Utah

DECEMBER 4 South Dakota

DECEMBER 12 Colorado

FEBRUARY 7 Nevada

SEPTEMBER 22 Alabama

JANUARY 28 South Carolina

JANUARY 27 Wyoming

Suffrage Convention Louisville, KY 1911

SEPTEMBER 10 New Hampshire

SEPTEMBER 8 Minnesota

AUGUST 2 Montana & Nebraska

JULY 28 Arkansas

"...this article by appropriate legislation."

...count of sex. Congress shall have power to enforce

THE ROAD TO 36

After years of fighting and several failed attempts, Congress finally passed the Nineteenth Amendment in 1919—in the House of Representatives on May 21 and in the Senate on June 4. But the battle for the vote wasn't over. The legislatures in three-quarters of the states would also have to vote to ratify the amendment before it would officially become part of the US Constitution. The race to 36 was on.

"The right of citizens of the United States to vote shall not be denied or abridged by the United States or by any state

JUNE 16
Kansas, New York & Ohio

Your local paper publishes an editorial telling legislators not to vote for suffrage. **Go back 3 spaces.**

JUNE 24
Pennsylvania

JUNE 25
Massachusetts

MARCH 22
Washington

Feb. 12: Arizona approves the amendment, but Virginia rejects it. If you rolled a 4 or higher, you have enough votes! You can stay in Arizona! If you rolled a 3 or below, you're in Virginia. Lose a turn.

MARCH 29
Mississippi

AUGUST 18, 1920
Tennessee becomes the thirty-sixth state to ratify the Nineteenth Amendment! Suffrage would be the law of the land.

JUNE 28
Texas

Feb. 14: The League of Women Voters is founded in Chicago. **Go forward 2 spaces and celebrate!**

MARCH 10
West Virginia

FEBRUARY 28
Oklahoma

FEBRUARY 21
New Mexico

JUNE 2
Delaware

JULY 1
Louisiana

Dozens of people gather to hear your pro-suffrage speech in the town square! **Go forward 4 spaces.**

FEBRUARY 24
Maryland

JULY 2
Iowa

JULY 3
Missouri

JULY 24
Georgia

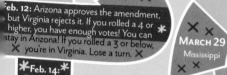

VOTES FOR WOMEN

VICTORY

To play this game, you'll need one die and a token for each player.

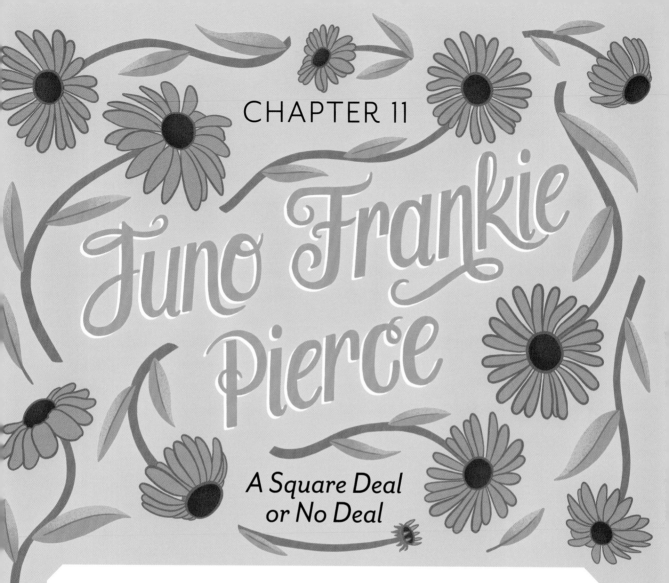

CHAPTER 11

Juno Frankie Pierce

A Square Deal or No Deal

After Congress finally passed the Nineteenth Amendment in 1919, the fight for women's suffrage moved to the individual states. In order for the amendment to officially become part of the Constitution, the legislators in three-fourths of states also had to pass it. Back then there were just forty-eight states, so the amendment needed the backing of thirty-six of them. By the summer of 1920, thirty-five states around the country had ratified the amendment. The finish line was in sight.

Of the remaining states, Tennessee seemed the most promising. The amendment had been approved by Tennessee's Senate and now awaited a vote from its House of Representatives.

Tennessee was thrown into the national spotlight. People from all over the country descended on Nashville, the capital, to express their opinions. For. Against. For. Against.

There were protests and marches and heated conversations. The mood became urgent. Tennessee could decide the fate of women across the country.

Now before the Tennessee legislature considered the Nineteenth Amendment, it voted in April 1919 to give women the right to vote in local and presidential elections. The leaders of the suffrage movement decided to use the local elections beginning that spring—the first ones in which women could go to the ballot box—to demonstrate just how enthusiastic women were about participating in the democratic process. In order to convince lawmakers to give women the vote, they needed to show that they would use it once they had it. With all eyes on Tennessee, the pressure was on to bring as many women as possible to the polls.

One of Nashville's most well-known suffrage strategists at the time was Catherine Talty Kenny, who had a plan to get out the vote. In Tennessee, as in many other states, black women were barred from joining white suffrage organizations. But Catherine, who was white, knew that in this fight they would be stronger if they worked together, that they couldn't let societal prejudices or racial segregation get in their way. To secure this right for all women, she would form historic partnerships with black organizers in the city, including a woman named Juno Frankie Pierce.

Frankie was the president of the Nashville Federation of Colored Women's Clubs, a civil rights organization that she helped start in the early 1900s. Catherine had heard about Frankie's leadership and her successful fight for such rights

Pro-suffrage ribbon. 1915.

Tennessee
Equal Suffrage
Ass'n.
━━━
8th Annual
Convention
━━━
Chattanooga
Dec. 9, 1915.

as access to public restrooms for the members of her community. Both Catherine and Frankie understood the power of voting as a tool to advocate for issues they cared about.

That summer, Catherine came to Frankie with a proposal: meet with the members of her group. Join forces to turn out the vote. And maybe they could find a way to help each other.

Frankie knew that some white women were uninterested in—or even opposed to—black women's rights. But others, like Catherine, wanted the support of black women to strengthen their numbers in advocating for the right to vote. And Frankie wanted something in return.

A friend of hers, who was a probation officer, had told her about a problem he'd noticed in the state. When white girls in Tennessee got into trouble with the law, they were sent to a vocational school, where they got an education and special training. But black students weren't allowed in this white school, and there wasn't a separate facility for them. Instead, when black girls got into trouble, they were sent to jail.

Frankie, who worked as a schoolteacher, had a different idea. These girls were still so young, and they had so much potential. They needed attention and guidance and good teachers.

They needed their own school.

Frankie needed support to create her school—and she would leverage her role in the suffrage movement to get it.

Through the summer, black and white women in Nashville worked together for their common goal, registering thousands of women voters, about a third of whom were black. Frankie and her friend Dr. Mattie E. Coleman, one of the first African American physicians in the state, spearheaded the efforts to work with black churches and other organizations in the area to help women register, getting 2,500 black women on the voting rolls.

After their successes in 1919, the Nashville suffragists turned their full attention to the Nineteenth Amendment. Once again, Catherine needed Frankie and Mattie's help to get suffrage over the finish line. And they were ready to ask for the white women's help in return.

Catherine invited Frankie to speak at the first meeting of the newly formed League of Women Voters of Tennessee. On May 18, 1920, Frankie entered the capitol building's House chambers—an imposing room with high ceilings, stone columns, and stately chandeliers. After her introduction, she took the podium and looked at the faces around the room. Everyone appeared rapt, waiting for her to speak.

She cleared her throat and began her speech with a pledge to continue working with the white women. "We are interested in the same moral uplift of the community in which we live as you are," she said. "We are asking only one thing—a square deal."

"WE ARE ASKING ONLY ONE THING— A SQUARE DEAL."

She paused for a moment, her words hanging in the air with a degree of suspense.

"We want recognition in all forms of government," she continued. "We want a state vocational school and a child welfare department of the state, and more room in state schools."

The white women agreed to support her requests.

A few more months of conversations and planning went by. Then it was August 18, the day the Tennessee House was going to vote.

The House chambers were abuzz with lawmakers and onlookers. Photographers were posted nearby to capture the moment. Roses were pinned to the

lapels of nearly everyone in attendance—yellow meant "yes, ratify!" and red meant "no."

Among those voting was a young lawmaker named Harry T. Burn, who was wearing a red rose. No one expected him to vote yes. But he had received a letter from his mother, Phoebe, who was a supporter of the suffragist Carrie Chapman Catt. In it, she told her son, "Be a good boy and help Mrs. Catt put the 'rat' in ratification."

When he was called on, he said "aye" so quickly that for a second no one reacted. Then the chamber erupted. It was a decisive vote! The Nineteenth Amendment would pass, 50–46.

Women in the chamber jumped up and down and hugged one another. The anti-suffrage lawmakers all shouted their disagreement. Harry snuck out the back.

Three years later, the Tennessee Vocational School for Colored Girls opened, with a huge campus near the Tennessee Agricultural and Industrial State Normal School in Nashville. The school welcomed girls ages twelve to fifteen from courts across the state. Frankie was its first superintendent.

Frankie retired in 1939, but the school continued to flourish and even began accepting girls at the elementary level. It was racially integrated in 1966, years after Frankie's death in 1954. By then she was recognized as an educator, civil rights leader, and visionary who had helped better the world.

Front page of The San Francisco Call *on August 18, 1920— the day Tennessee ratified the Nineteenth Amendment.*

CHAPTER 12

Susette La Flesche Tibbles

Speaking Up for Her People

As we learned from the Haudenosaunee, Native women were active participants in their own tribal governments long before other women in America had even dreamed of winning equal representation.

Yet even after the Nineteenth Amendment was ratified, in 1920, states continued to deny Native men and women suffrage. The first people in the land that we now call the United States, from societies where women often had real political power, were among the last people to get the right to vote in America. They were pushed from their homelands and confined to reservations—often barren, harsh regions with few resources. They were denied full citizenship and separated from their traditional ways of life.

But even so, Native women were deeply engaged in the national battle for women's rights. One of the most well-known Native activists was Susette La Flesche Tibbles. Her fight for the rights of Native Americans expanded the idea of citizenship and helped lay the groundwork for women's suffrage.

Susette was born in 1854, a member of the Omaha tribe in what is now the state of Nebraska. From an early age, she learned the value of a good education from her father, Joseph La Flesche, who was the tribe's chief. He made sure that Susette learned not only the Omaha language but also English, because he knew she would need it to thrive in the new America. It quickly became apparent that she had a real talent for words: when she was still in high school, one of her essays was even published in a New York newspaper.

Susette La Flesche Tibbles. Circa 1879.

But no matter how smart Susette was, she knew that she couldn't rely on brains alone to make her dreams come true—not as a girl, and especially not as a Native girl. That became particularly clear when, after graduating from school in 1875, she tried to become a teacher on the Omaha Reservation.

Although Native Americans were supposed to be given priority to teach on the reservations, a white government official told Susette that she wasn't qualified: she didn't have a teaching certificate. She was sure she could pass the necessary tests, but there were no schools on the reservation that offered the certification exams, and

Native Americans at the time couldn't leave their reservations without the government's permission. When Susette asked the official if she could travel to a nearby school to take the tests, he refused. But she wasn't about to give up.

Borrowing one of her father's horses, she snuck off the reservation, riding nearly thirty miles to the city of Tekamah, where she made the school superintendent give her the tests. She passed and rode back home with her certificate, but the official still refused to budge. Finally, after she threatened to tell local newspapers about the discrimination, he gave in and issued her a teaching license. She became the first Native teacher on the Omaha Reservation.

Susette clearly had the courage and the smarts to fight for change, but her big jump into activism didn't come until seven years later. In her early twenties, she traveled with her father to visit another tribe, the Ponca, in Oklahoma. The Ponca people had been forced there by the US government after being kicked out of their longtime home in Nebraska. Their new home was completely inhospitable. They had been given no food, shelter, or supplies, and they arrived too late in the season to plant any new crops. In their first winter, many of the tribe's members died of illness or starvation. Susette was horrified. The American government had betrayed its promises to the Ponca people, and someone had to fight back. And that someone, Susette realized, could be her.

Before long, she got her chance. Around the time of her visit, the chief of the Ponca, Standing Bear, was detained after trying to return to Nebraska. Standing Bear hadn't received permission from white officials to leave the reservation, but he had gone anyway. His son had just died, and his son's last wish had been to be buried in his homeland. The government arrested Standing Bear and locked him up in a military fort.

Many people saw this as horribly unjust, and a newspaper editor named Thomas Tibbles suggested that Standing Bear bring his case to a judge. But there was one big problem: the chief didn't speak English. So Susette agreed to

Standing Bear, chief of the Ponca. 1877.

translate for him, even though she was very shy at the time.

With Susette's help, the chief delivered an emotional speech about how Native Americans were just as human as white Americans. He stood up and gestured with his right hand. "That hand is not the color of yours, but if I pierce it, I shall feel pain," he said. "If you pierce your hand, you also feel pain. The blood that will flow from mine will be of the same color as yours. I am a man. The same God made us both." Susette relayed his words, and together, she and Standing Bear made the court-room audience weep.

Amazingly for the time period, Standing Bear won his case. In 1879, a judge ruled that a Native American counted as a "person" under the law—a right that hadn't been recognized until then—and that Native Americans were entitled to "life, liberty and the pursuit of happiness." The victory was not explicitly connected to voting rights—and it didn't mean that they were citizens—but it was a big step in that direction. By declaring that Native Americans should have legal rights, too, Susette had helped expand the idea of who could be an American and what that meant.

And that was just the start. Susette and Standing Bear toured the East Coast, speaking to large crowds about Native American culture and rights. They later traveled to England and Scotland, where they spoke to rich and powerful British people, including lords and ladies. Thomas Tibbles, the newspaper editor, came, too. By then, he and Susette were married. Susette was much more than just a translator during these tours. She overcame her shyness and gave her own speeches, and newspaper accounts of her appearances quickly brought her fame.

> "THAT HAND IS NOT THE COLOR OF YOURS, BUT IF I PIERCE IT, I SHALL FEEL PAIN. IF YOU PIERCE YOUR HAND, YOU ALSO FEEL PAIN. THE BLOOD THAT WILL FLOW FROM MINE WILL BE OF THE SAME COLOR AS YOURS. I AM A MAN. THE SAME GOD MADE US BOTH."

For the rest of her life, she never stopped speaking up for her people. She became a journalist, writing about white settlers' violence against Native Americans and other discriminatory treatment. Because of her work, new audiences across the country—and around the world—learned about the abuse of Native Americans and joined in efforts to help end injustice.

But for all the success and recognition Susette achieved, the struggle for Native Americans and Native women continued. Even as she was touring and speaking, families and tribes were being forced from their land and relocated to faraway reservations. Children were being taken to missionary schools and stripped of their traditions. It would be another generation before full recognition and suffrage was granted to Native Americans, and it would require others taking up Susette's mission for it to happen.

CHAPTER 13

Zitkála-Šá Opens the Door

ZITKÁLA-ŠÁ'S LIFE CHANGED FOREVER WHEN SHE WAS EIGHT YEARS OLD, THE DAY the white missionaries came to the Dakota Sioux reservation where she lived.

Before that, she was learning to sew beads onto moccasins, listening to tribal elders tell myths in her mother's wigwam home, and celebrating battle victories at feasts with her neighbors. "I was as free as the wind that blew my hair, and no less spirited than a bounding deer," she later wrote.

But the missionaries who came in 1884 wanted to take Native children to a school where they would learn English and become "civilized." Zitkála-Šá was too young to know any better, and she eagerly agreed. She thought the plan seemed like a grand adventure. She had never seen a train before, and she was excited to ride on what she called an "iron horse."

But her excitement didn't last long. When she got to the school, in Indiana, she found that the teachers spoke a strange language and wore strange clothes. She wasn't allowed to sing her family songs or talk about her tribe's traditions. The worst part came when they forced her to cut her hair: for the Dakota Sioux, short hair was a sign of mourning or cowardice.

Zitkála-Šá was alone, scared, and angry, far from her family and loved ones. Even years later, after she had learned English, finished school, and become an accomplished writer, pianist, and violinist, she remembered that fear and loneliness. She knew that white people didn't see her as equal, but she didn't understand why she should be less important just because she was not white. Wasn't *she* American too? And who gave them the right to decide what was the "right" way to live and speak and dress? Her family was here first, and they'd

Female students at the Carlisle Indian Industrial School in Pennsylvania—one of numerous boarding schools operated by the Bureau of Indian Affairs to forcibly "Americanize" Native children. Circa late nineteenth century.

been dressing themselves and talking and getting along just fine before the white settlers came and started telling them how to live, where to make their homes, and what language to speak.

In an essay, she described her life's goal: "We would open the door of American opportunity to the red man and encourage him to find his rightful place in our American life."

Starting in her twenties, Zitkála-Šá—who sometimes went by her English name, Gertrude Simmons Bonnin—joined and founded several Native American rights groups. She edited a Native American magazine that called for citizenship rights. She even moved to Washington, DC, where she continued to work for the fair treatment of Native people.

Zitkála-Šá. Circa 1898.

She also knew that women and Native Americans shared a common goal—defeating discrimination—and that the two groups would be stronger if they fought it together. So, in addition to joining Native American activist groups, she joined a women's rights organization—and then started a Native American committee within it, saying, "Now the time is at hand when the American Indian shall have his day in court through the help of the women of America."

> ## "NOW THE TIME IS AT HAND WHEN THE AMERICAN INDIAN SHALL HAVE HIS DAY IN COURT THROUGH THE HELP OF THE WOMEN OF AMERICA."

Yet the winning of the vote for women in 1920 didn't mean that every Native woman could vote. Many Native Americans, men and women, were still not considered US citizens. But four years later, in 1924, Zitkála-Šá's work led to a considerable victory when Congress passed the Indian Citizenship Act, which recognized all Native Americans as citizens. Not all Native people wanted to participate in American politics—they had their own tribal governments—but this meant that, in theory, they were entitled to equal voting rights.

But Zitkála-Šá wanted more than voting rights. She wanted to share the beauty of Native American culture with the world. She had written a book called *Old Indian Legends,* an anthology in which she retold stories she had heard as a child. She had also written *The Sun Dance Opera*—the first opera by a Native American. It told the love story of Winona, the daughter of a Sioux chief, and Ohiya, a tribal warrior. Their romance grows around the Sioux sun dance, one of the tribal rituals the American government had banned.

The fight to guarantee Native rights continued long after these struggles.

Cover of Old Indian Legends
by Zitkála-Šá. 1901.

Cover of American Indian Stories
by Zitkála-Šá. 1921.

Immediately after the Indian Citizenship Act was passed, several states wrote new laws banning Native Americans from voting. Those laws stayed in place for decades. Even today, some states have restrictions that make it difficult for Native Americans to vote, even though limiting a specific group's voting rights is illegal. In 2018, the Supreme Court allowed a North Dakota law to go into effect requiring voters to have their home address on their ID cards. Since lots of Native American reservations don't have street signs or house numbers, this meant that many Native people couldn't vote.

Still, as others have tried to take away their rights, Native Americans have fought tirelessly to protect them. In the early 1960s in South Dakota, Native American voters turned out in huge numbers to block a law that would have given the government control of their land. And in North Dakota, facing the 2018 law, tribal leaders worked day and night to issue new ID cards for their people so they could vote in that year's midterm elections.

Zitkála-Šá knew that even as the United States grew in size and power, it was critical to the future of all Americans that they recognize and remember all the nations within this nation. As she wrote in the preface to *Old Indian Legends,* "I have tried to transplant the native spirit of these tales—root and all—into the English language, since America in the last few centuries has acquired a second tongue."

Anna Julia Cooper, an orator, author, and educator who was active in the black women's club movement at the turn of the century. Her 1892 book, A Voice From the South by a Black Woman of the South, is considered a foundational black feminist text. Circa 1902.

CONCLUSION

FINISH THE FIGHT

ON ELECTION DAY IN 1920, IN CITIES AND TOWNS ACROSS THE UNITED STATES, they came to the polls. Young and old, in cars and on foot, on their way to the grocery store or on their lunch breaks, the women of America made their way to the ballot box. Some of them, "expecting a long wait in the lines, brought along their luncheons," *The New York Times* reported. Eighty-three women from a nursing home in Manhattan even "walked to the polling place two blocks away, refusing to ride in automobiles. Twenty-five of their number were more than 90 years old." At some polling places, women outnumbered the men. And at the Women's City Club, all three floors were packed with women waiting to hear the results of their first presidential election as voters. It was, *The Times* declared, the "largest vote on record."

But it wasn't a celebration everywhere.

All across the South, where most African Americans lived, black women and men who tried to vote were harassed and intimidated. In some places, they made it to the polls only to be refused ballots.

The Ku Klux Klan (KKK), a white-supremacist organization that terrorized African Americans and other minority groups, had been founded after the Civil War and disbanded a few years later, but by 1920, the organization was resurging. And they were committed to keeping newly enfranchised voters away from the polls.

In Miami, the KKK put up posters declaring "Beware! The Ku Klux Klan is again alive! And every Negro who approaches a polling place next Tuesday will be a marked man." This threat was surely not limited to men.

In Lake City, a small town in northern Florida, a black man who had led classes instructing black women on how to fill out the ballot was dragged from his bed in the middle of the night, had a noose tied around his neck, and was driven several miles away before he was able to escape.

And in November 1920, the suffragist and educator Mary McLeod Bethune found out how far the nation still had to go in giving all women their rights.

Mary had started a school for African American women in Daytona, Florida, and the night before the landmark election, a local faction of the KKK showed up to scare her and her students away from voting.

Undeterred, Mary stood on the quad with her arms folded and her head held high. She began to sing the words of a stirring hymn: "Be not dismayed whate'er betide, God will take care of you."

The Klansmen retreated. And Mary bravely went to the polls the next morning to cast her vote—along with ten million other American women.

Mary, who would later be known as the First Lady of Black America, spent her whole life working to make the United States more equal for everyone. And her story is just one of thousands. "We have fought for America with all her imperfections, not so much for what she is, but for what we know she can be," she said.

> "WE HAVE FOUGHT FOR AMERICA WITH ALL HER IMPERFECTIONS, NOT SO MUCH FOR WHAT SHE IS, BUT FOR WHAT WE KNOW SHE CAN BE."

Mary McLeod Bethune with students from the Daytona Literary and Industrial Training School for Negro Girls. Circa 1905.

But the struggle to access the ballot continued. And African Americans and Native Americans weren't the only ones fighting for the right to vote.

In 1929, the legislature of Puerto Rico, a US territory, granted women the right to vote in territorial elections—but only if they passed a literacy test, which was a way to keep poor and working-class women away from the polls. The literacy requirement wouldn't be lifted until 1935.

In 1943, Chinese immigrants were permitted to become citizens—and, if they did, to vote—with the repeal of the Chinese Exclusion Act, which had kept such women as Mabel Ping-Hua Lee from voting.

In the 1950s and 1960s, civil rights activists struggled to end segregation—to strike down the "separate but equal" laws that kept white Americans apart from black Americans. Voting rights came to the fore again. In the Constitution, African Americans had the right to vote, but in reality, suppression and violent intimidation kept millions from the polls.

Leaders such as Fannie Lou Hamer demanded that the nation make good on the promises of the Fifteenth and Nineteenth Amendments. She joined the brave ranks of activists who worked to help register people to vote. As she said at the

Fannie Lou Hamer, at left, with her fellow Mississippi-based civil rights activists
Victoria Gray Adams and Annie Devine in front of the US Capitol. 1965.

time, "The only thing they could do to me was to kill me and it seemed like they'd been trying to do that a little bit at a time ever since I could remember."

Fannie and activists like her helped pass the Voting Rights Act of 1965, which prohibited racial discrimination in voting. That law made the promise of the Nineteenth Amendment a reality for millions of women of color, and many historians see it as the conclusion of the suffrage movement. But it was not the end of the fight for equality.

It's a fight that women politicians, with the support of the women voters who helped elect them, have led. Among them was Representative Patsy Takemoto Mink, who in 1964 became the first woman of color elected to the US Congress.

As a young woman growing up in Hawaii, Patsy, the granddaughter of Japanese American immigrants, wanted to be a doctor, but she was turned down by every medical school she applied to. As a member of Congress, she fought to make sure that others would not have the same experience. In 1972, she was the lead author of Title IX, a law that said that schools receiving federal funding could not discriminate on the basis of sex.

Today, the law is most famous for opening the door for millions of girls and women to play sports, but it applied equally to academics. And in 1974, Patsy also spearheaded the Women's Educational Equity Act, which, among other things, called for an end to gender stereotypes in textbooks and school lessons.

We hope this book honors that goal and the broader fight for equality that Patsy and countless other women have been part of. "It is easy enough to vote right and consistently be with the majority," Patsy said in a 1975 speech. "But it is more often more important to be ahead of the majority and this means we must be willing to cut the first furrow in the ground and stand alone for a while if necessary."

Representative Patsy Takemoto Mink, Democrat, of Hawaii, with a homemade nameplate for her new office. 1965.

AUTHORS' NOTE

When we asked the question "What don't we know about suffrage?" the answer was *a lot*. Knowing that the right to vote is a cornerstone of American citizenship, we wanted to create a history of suffrage that gave voice to the diverse group of American women who made it happen. We wanted to talk not only about the better-known women in American history—such as Susan B. Anthony and Elizabeth Cady Stanton—but also women like Jovita Idár, Juno Frankie Pierce, and Zitkála-Šá.

It became clear pretty quickly that suffrage was not a movement that was happening in isolation. Many of the early suffragists, both black and white, were part of the movement to abolish slavery, which inspired them to start thinking about women's equality too. At the same time, Native American women and men were fighting to protect their land rights and their own traditions while also claiming equal citizenship as Americans. By the late nineteenth century, debates over immigration and the rights of workers were also coming to the fore. Temperance, a movement to limit or prohibit the consumption of alcohol, gets woven into the suffrage movement too because some women saw temperance laws as a way of protecting women from domestic violence stemming from alcohol abuse. Without the right to vote, it was hard for women to protect themselves. As Ida B. Wells-Barnett wrote, "In nearly all communities wife beating is punishable with a fine, and in no community is it made a felony."

Perhaps the most important thing we were reminded of was that laws and rights are never won once and for all. Laws that feel essential to equality can be changed. Hard-won rights can be taken away. Which goes straight to the central theme of this book: voting is power.

One of the most interesting things we learned while working on this book was that way before 1920, women did vote in this country. On Election Day in 1868, a group of women showed up at the polling place in Vineland, New Jersey, with a homemade ballot box that they'd cobbled together from blueberry crates. They set it up across from the building that held the real ballot box. And one by one, 172 women, white and black, paraded by to cast their symbolic votes for president.

Their protest was soon followed by similar ones across the country. But this didn't come out of nowhere. In fact, in the decades after the American Revolution, women in New Jersey had voted—for real.

The Declaration of Independence famously said that "all men are created equal," but most new state constitutions written at the time of the Revolution said that only "freemen" or "white male inhabitants" could vote. New Jersey, however, was different. Its constitution, written in 1776, granted the vote to all free "inhabitants," regardless of gender or race, as long as "they"—lawmakers used that gender-neutral pronoun—had been in in their county for at least a year and could declare they had £50 worth of property to their name.

It was a sizable but not exorbitant sum. And it ruled out married women, who by law had to surrender any property or income to their husbands. But, according to historians, a significant number of single, property-holding New Jersey women did manage to vote. And it wasn't just white women who could vote, a fact not lost on many New Jerseyites. In a letter to a newspaper written in 1800, one lawmaker made things plain. "Our constitution gives this right to maids and widows, white and black," he wrote.

Not all politicians were happy about that, especially when women voted for rival candidates. New Jersey elections, like a lot of elections in early America, were often chaotic, corrupt, and intensely partisan. And when things got messy at the polls, guess who got the blame? Newspapers were full of stories about incompetent, easily manipulated "petticoat electors."

Things came to a head in 1806 during a bitterly fought election to decide where a county courthouse would be built. Nearly fourteen thousand votes were cast—far more than the number of voters in the county! Once again, the finger was pointed at women, African Americans, and even "people from Philadelphia." (Yes, there was interstate trash-talking long before professional sports.) In 1807, the New Jersey constitution was changed to say that only white men could vote.

Decades later, in 1880, Elizabeth Cady Stanton went to the polling place in Tenafly, New Jersey, where she was living, to lay her ballot on top of the ballot box, daring the poll official to deprive her of her citizen's right. "There are many precedents for women voting," Elizabeth declared, reminding him of America's real history. "On the sacred soil of New Jersey where we now stand, women voted."

The story of women voting in New Jersey became a half-forgotten historical footnote. But suffragists did not forget. We wrote this book to be part of the remembering—of the importance of this decades-long struggle for equality and the inspiring women who changed the course of history by fighting tirelessly for the rights of American citizenship.

TIMELINE

1807

New Jersey amends its election laws, limiting voting rights to white, property-owning men only.

1869

Congress passes the Fifteenth Amendment, declaring that black men have the right to vote. Three-quarters of the states must ratify it before it becomes law.

The Wyoming Territory becomes the first in the United States where women can vote. Officials in Wyoming stand up for women's suffrage, even when it later threatens their petition for statehood. "We will remain out of the Union one hundred years rather than come in without the women," they reportedly say in a telegram to Congress.

Frederick Douglass with his wife Helen Pitts Douglass, seated, and her sister Eva Pitts. Late nineteenth century.

1848

Suffragists including Elizabeth Cady Stanton, Lucretia Mott, and Frederick Douglass meet in upstate New York for the landmark Seneca Falls Convention to discuss women's rights. They put their ideas into a document called the Declaration of Sentiments.

1850

1860

1870

1832

Maria W. Stewart—an African American abolitionist and one of the first American women to speak publicly about politics to audiences of mixed races and genders—gives a speech in Boston decrying the treatment of black women.

1861–1865

During the Civil War, eleven Southern states secede from the United States because they don't want to give up their right to own enslaved people. The North wins, slavery is abolished, and the Southern states return to the Union.

1851

At a women's rights convention in Akron, Ohio, the formerly enslaved abolitionist and suffragist Sojourner Truth delivers a famous speech about women's rights. "I have plowed and reaped and husked and chopped and mowed, and can any man do more than that?" she asks the crowd. "I have heard much about the sexes being equal. . . . I am as strong as any man that is now."

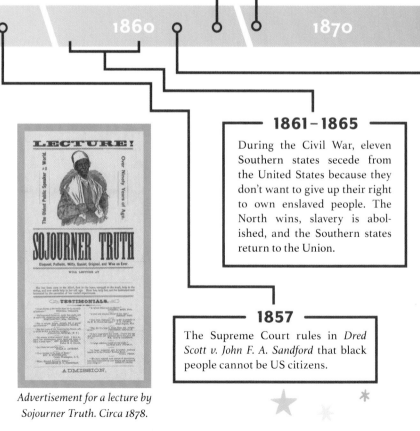

Advertisement for a lecture by Sojourner Truth. Circa 1878.

1857

The Supreme Court rules in *Dred Scott v. John F. A. Sandford* that black people cannot be US citizens.

1870

On February 3, 1870, Iowa becomes the twenty-eighth state to ratify the Fifteenth Amendment. In March, President Ulysses S. Grant writes a special message to Congress, urging them to take the matter of racial equality seriously: "To the race more favored heretofore by our laws I would say, Withhold no legal privilege of advancement to the new citizen." Nevertheless, white people with power in the South soon devise tactics to prevent black people—and poorer white people—from voting.

Women in the Utah Territory get the vote.

1890

Two major women's rights groups merge to form the National American Woman Suffrage Association (NAWSA), which leads the fight for suffrage laws on the state and federal levels.

Josephine St. Pierre Ruffin starts *The Woman's Era,* the first newspaper in the United States founded by a black woman.

1882

Congress passes the Chinese Exclusion Act, which bars Chinese workers from entering the United States and prevents those in the country from becoming citizens.

1893

Women win the right to vote in Colorado.

1880   1890   1900

1866

Those fighting for black people's right to vote and those fighting for women's right to vote join forces to form the American Equal Rights Association. The group's goal is "to secure Equal Rights to all American citizens, especially the right of suffrage, irrespective of race, color, or sex." That year, the first of many petitions for a universal suffrage amendment granting voting rights to all citizens—male and female—is presented to Congress.

1896

The Supreme Court rules in *Plessy v. Ferguson,* establishing the doctrine of "separate but equal" that opens the door to Jim Crow laws and institutional segregation across the country.

Excluded by many white suffrage groups, black suffragists—including Mary Church Terrell, Ida B. Wells-Barnett, and Frances Ellen Watkins Harper—form their own group, the National Association of Colored Women (NACW), which continues to fight for equal rights today.

Women in Idaho win the right to vote.

The Phyllis Wheatley Club, an affiliate of the NACW in Buffalo, New York. Early twentieth century.

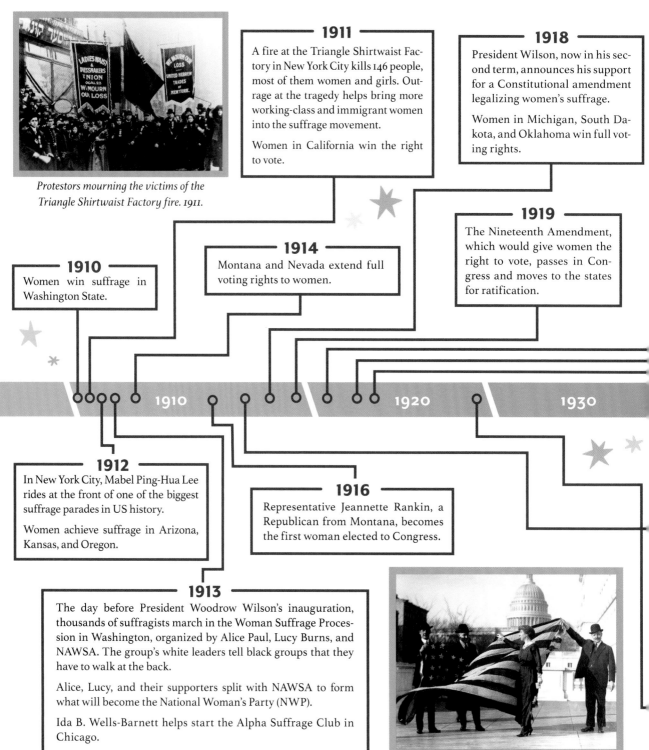

1911

A fire at the Triangle Shirtwaist Factory in New York City kills 146 people, most of them women and girls. Outrage at the tragedy helps bring more working-class and immigrant women into the suffrage movement.

Women in California win the right to vote.

Protestors mourning the victims of the Triangle Shirtwaist Factory fire. 1911.

1918

President Wilson, now in his second term, announces his support for a Constitutional amendment legalizing women's suffrage.

Women in Michigan, South Dakota, and Oklahoma win full voting rights.

1919

The Nineteenth Amendment, which would give women the right to vote, passes in Congress and moves to the states for ratification.

1910

Women win suffrage in Washington State.

1914

Montana and Nevada extend full voting rights to women.

1910

1920

1930

1912

In New York City, Mabel Ping-Hua Lee rides at the front of one of the biggest suffrage parades in US history.

Women achieve suffrage in Arizona, Kansas, and Oregon.

1916

Representative Jeannette Rankin, a Republican from Montana, becomes the first woman elected to Congress.

1913

The day before President Woodrow Wilson's inauguration, thousands of suffragists march in the Woman Suffrage Procession in Washington, organized by Alice Paul, Lucy Burns, and NAWSA. The group's white leaders tell black groups that they have to walk at the back.

Alice, Lucy, and their supporters split with NAWSA to form what will become the National Woman's Party (NWP).

Ida B. Wells-Barnett helps start the Alpha Suffrage Club in Chicago.

Women win the right to vote in Illinois and the Alaska Territory.

Congresswoman Jeannette Rankin being presented with a flag at the Capitol. Circa 1918.

1920

On August 18, Tennessee becomes the thirty-sixth state to vote yes on the Nineteenth Amendment. It is certified by the Secretary of State on August 26, making it law. American women nationwide now have the right to vote, but in many places, when black women go to the polls, people try to stop them. Many Latinas, Asian women, and Native women are also excluded.

1923

Texas passes a "white primary" law, barring African Americans from voting in the primaries of the Democratic Party, which dominates the state.

The Equal Rights Amendment, written by Alice Paul, is introduced in Congress. It declares: "Men and women shall have equal rights throughout the United States and every place subject to its jurisdiction."

Pro-suffrage pin.
Early twentieth century.

1924

The Indian Citizenship Act declares that all Native Americans born in the United States are citizens.

1943

The Chinese Exclusion Act is repealed, opening up the possibility of citizenship—and voting rights—to Chinese immigrants.

1940   **1950**   **1960**

1917

Members of the NWP who call themselves the Silent Sentinels begin picketing outside the White House. Over the next two years, many are eventually arrested—some are beaten and abused—but they continue their protest.

Women achieve voting rights victories in New York, North Dakota, Arkansas, and Nebraska. Indiana also passes a law granting women limited voting rights, but it is struck down by the state's supreme court a few months later.

1965

Congress passes the Voting Rights Act, which bans racial discrimination in elections. It outlaws literacy tests and other barriers to voting and sets up federal supervision of states with a history of discriminatory voting practices.

1972

Congress passes the Equal Rights Amendment, which moves to the states for ratification. As of the writing of this book, its fate is still uncertain.

1929

Puerto Rican women win the right to vote in territorial elections—but only if they satisfy a literacy requirement, which is not lifted until 1935.

Fannie Lou Hamer speaking outside the US Capitol on September 17, 1965.

BRAVE AND REVOLUTIONARY WOMEN YOU SHOULD KNOW

BLANCHE AMES AMES, 1878–1969, MASSACHUSETTS: artist, botanical illustrator, and member of the Massachusetts Woman Suffrage Association who advocated for women's voting and reproductive rights. She used her artistic talents to draw and publish pro-suffrage political cartoons.

SUSAN B. ANTHONY, 1820–1906, NEW YORK: cofounder of the American Equal Rights Association (AERA), the National Woman Suffrage Association (NWSA), and the National American Woman Suffrage Association (NAWSA). The Nineteenth Amendment is sometimes called the Anthony Amendment in her honor.

MARIE LOUISE BOTTINEAU BALDWIN, 1863–1952, CHIPPEWA OF NORTH DAKOTA: moved to Washington, DC, to defend the treaty rights of the Métis Turtle Mountain Band of the Chippewa Nation. A member of the Society of American Indians, she marched in the 1913 Woman Suffrage Procession in Washington and testified before Congress for Native rights and suffrage.

MARY MCLEOD BETHUNE, 1875–1955, FLORIDA: founding president of the National Council of Negro Women, vice president of the National Association for the Advancement of Colored People (NAACP), and the so-called First Lady of Black America, who was a member of President Franklin D. Roosevelt's unofficial "Black Cabinet," a group of African Americans who served as public policy advisers.

AMELIA BLOOMER, 1818–1894, NEW YORK: founder and editor of *The Lily,* one of the first newspapers made by and for women in the United States. She was also an advocate for dress reform, lending its supporters' signature attire—bloomers—her name.

MARY BURRILL, 1881–1946, DISTRICT OF COLUMBIA: playwright, teacher, and prominent member of the community of black suffragists in Washington, who is believed to have been romantically involved with Angelina Weld Grimké as a teenager. As an adult, her partner was Lucy Diggs Slowe.

MARY ANN SHADD CARY, 1823–1893, DISTRICT OF COLUMBIA/CANADA: founder of the Colored Women's Progressive Franchise Association and the first black woman to publish a newspaper in North America.

CARRIE CHAPMAN CATT, 1859–1947, IOWA/NEW YORK: president of NAWSA who developed the "Winning Plan" that led to the ratification of the Nineteenth Amendment and cofounder of the League of Women Voters. Her partner was Mary Garrett Hay.

DR. MATTIE E. COLEMAN, 1870–1943, TENNESSEE: one of the first black female physicians in Tennessee, who partnered with white suffragists in the fight for the Nineteenth Amendment.

CORALIE FRANKLIN COOK, 1861–1942, VIRGINIA: a founder of the National Association of Colored Women (NACW). She eventually left the suffrage movement because she felt it had abandoned black women.

ANA ROQUÉ DE DUPREY, 1853–1933, PUERTO RICO: founder of the Puerto Rican Feminist League and the Puerto Rican Association of Women Suffragists, which fought against literacy tests and other impediments to voting. She also started *La Mujer,* the first women's magazine in Puerto Rico.

DR. CORA SMITH EATON, 1867–1939, WASHINGTON: physician and mountaineer, who was the first woman to climb the East Peak of Mount Olympus. She planted a Votes for Women banner on the top of Washington's Mount Rainier in 1909, a year before women in the state won the right to vote.

ELIZABETH PIPER ENSLEY, 1848–1919, COLORADO: cofounder of the Colorado Non-Partisan Equal Suffrage Association, Denver correspondent for *The Woman's Era,* and founder of the Colored Woman's Republican Club.

MATILDA JOSLYN GAGE, 1826–1898, NEW YORK: cofounder of the NWSA and coauthor of the "Declaration of Rights of Women of the United States." She was honorarily adopted as a member of the Wolf Clan of the Mohawk Nation.

ANGELINA WELD GRIMKÉ, 1880–1958, DISTRICT OF COLUMBIA: journalist, poet, and playwright who used her pen to advocate for civil rights and women's suffrage, and is believed to have been romantically involved with Mary Burrill as a teenager.

FRANCES ELLEN WATKINS HARPER, 1825–1911, MARYLAND/PENNSYLVANIA: prolific author, poet, orator, and co-founder of the American Woman Suffrage Association (AWSA) who helped organize and lead the NACW.

MARY GARRETT HAY, 1857–1928, NEW YORK: member of NAWSA who helped her partner, Carrie Chapman Catt, enact the "Winning Plan" to pass the Nineteenth Amendment. She later became the chair of the New York City League of Women Voters.

MARGARET HINCHEY, 1870–1944, IRELAND/NEW YORK: immigrant and leader of the Laundry Workers Union of New York. She met with President Woodrow Wilson to advocate for suffrage and helped organize working-class men and women to campaign for the vote.

VERA HOLME, 1881–1969, AND EVELINA HAVERFIELD, 1867–1920, BRITAIN: suffragists and romantic partners. Vera was the Pankhursts' chauffeur and a theater performer, and she earned the nickname "Jack" for wearing masculine clothing. Evelina served as a nurse in World War I.

JOVITA IDÁR, 1885–1946, TEXAS: journalist and newspaper publisher who advocated for women's suffrage and fair treatment for Mexican Americans in *El Progreso, La Crónica,* and *Evolución.* She helped found the League of Mexican Women and later worked as an election precinct judge.

ANNIE KENNEY, 1879–1953, BRITAIN: working-class woman who rose through the ranks of the Women's Social and Political Union (WSPU) in England and was imprisoned repeatedly for her activism.

CATHERINE TALTY KENNY, 1874–1950, TENNESSEE: leader of the ratification committee of the Tennessee Equal Suffrage League. She partnered with black suffragists in the fight for the Nineteenth Amendment.

MABEL PING-HUA LEE, 1896–1966, NEW YORK: first Chinese woman to earn a PhD from Columbia University. As a teenager, she led a 1912 suffrage parade in New York on horseback.

ADELLA HUNT LOGAN, 1863–1915, GEORGIA/ALABAMA: teacher at the Tuskegee Institute who was a member of NAWSA and NACW, wrote for *The Woman's Journal,* and fought for social reform, suffrage, and better health care for black communities.

LUCRETIA MOTT, 1793–1880, PENNSYLVANIA: first president of the AERA and an organizer of the Seneca Falls Convention. As part of a Quaker delegation, she visited the Haudenosaunee, who empowered women for centuries.

CAROLINE PARKER MOUNTPLEASANT, CA. 1824–1892, HAUDENOSAUNEE OF NEW YORK: Peace Queen of the Seneca Wolf Clan who served as a kind of cultural ambassador for the tribe. She is also known as Ga-hah-no.

EMMELINE PANKHURST, 1858–1928, BRITAIN: a leader of the suffrage movement in England and cofounder of the WSPU, which became known for its militant activism.

ALICE PAUL, 1885–1977, NEW JERSEY: cofounder of the National Woman's Party. She organized NAWSA's 1913 Woman Suffrage Procession in Washington, DC, led the Silent Sentinels' protest, and drafted the Equal Rights Amendment.

JUNO FRANKIE PIERCE, CA. 1862–1954, TENNESSEE: president of the Nashville Federation of Colored Women's Clubs who partnered with white suffragists in the fight for the Nineteenth Amendment and helped start the Tennessee Vocational School for Colored Girls.

HARRIET FORTEN PURVIS, 1810–1875, PENNSYLVANIA: suffrage advocate who established, with her mother, Charlotte Vandine Forten, and her sisters Margaretta and Sarah, the Philadelphia Female Anti-Slavery Society, the first abolitionist group for black and white women in the United States.

JEANNETTE RANKIN, 1880–1973, MONTANA: the first woman elected to Congress. She represented her home state as a Republican from 1917 to 1919 and from 1941 to 1943.

SARAH PARKER REMOND, 1824–1894, BRITAIN: American ex-pat who is believed to be the only black woman to sign the 1866 Women's Suffrage Petition, the first mass petition for women's right to vote presented to the British Parliament.

JOSEPHINE ST. PIERRE RUFFIN, 1842–1924, MASSACHUSETTS: founder and editor of *The Woman's Era,* the first newspaper in the United States started by a black woman. She also helped found the Boston chapter of the NAACP.

ROSE SCHNEIDERMAN, 1882–1972, POLAND/NEW YORK: immigrant and member of the International Ladies' Garment Workers Union, the Women's Trade Union League, and the Equality League of Self-Supporting Women. She advocated for women's and workers' rights, particularly in the aftermath of the Triangle Shirtwaist Factory fire.

DR. ANNA HOWARD SHAW, 1847–1919, MASSACHUSETTS: physician, minister, and powerful orator who served as president of NAWSA. Her partner was Lucy Anthony, the niece of Susan B. Anthony.

LUCY DIGGS SLOWE, 1885–1937, DISTRICT OF COLUMBIA: dean of women at Howard University and prominent member of the community of black suffragists in Washington. Her partner was Mary Burrill.

ELIZABETH CADY STANTON, 1815–1902, NEW YORK: organizer of the Seneca Falls Convention who was the main author of the Declaration of Sentiments. She also cofounded the AERA, NWSA, and NAWSA.

LUCY STONE, 1818–1893, MASSACHUSETTS: cofounder of the AERA, AWSA, and NAWSA. She was famous for keeping her last name when she married, leading other women who also kept their surnames to be dubbed "Lucy Stoners."

MARY CHURCH TERRELL, 1863–1954, DISTRICT OF COLUMBIA: founder of the Colored Women's League of Washington, first president of the NACW, and founding member of the NAACP.

SUSETTE LA FLESCHE TIBBLES, 1854–1903, OMAHA TRIBE OF NEBRASKA: teacher and journalist who acted as translator at the trial of Chief Standing Bear, which resulted in a federal ruling that Native Americans were "persons" under the law.

SOJOURNER TRUTH, CA. 1797–1883, NEW YORK/MICHIGAN: formerly enslaved person, abolitionist leader, and orator who famously spoke at the 1851 Women's Rights Convention in Akron, Ohio.

DR. MARY WALKER, 1832–1919, NEW YORK: field surgeon in the Union Army, advocate of dress reform, and the only woman to ever receive the Medal of Honor for service in wartime.

IDA B. WELLS-BARNETT, 1862–1931, ILLINOIS: journalist and cofounder of the Alpha Suffrage Club, a black women's organization in Chicago that fought for the vote. She marched with the Illinois delegation in the 1913 Woman Suffrage Procession in Washington and helped found the NACW and the National Negro Committee, which later became the NAACP.

VICTORIA WOODHULL, 1838–1927, NEW YORK: stockbroker and newspaper publisher who became the first woman to run for president of the United States.

FRANCES WRIGHT, 1795–1852, SCOTLAND/TENNESSEE: wealthy social reformer who advocated for suffrage, dress reform, and the abolition of slavery. She used her fortune to establish a commune for freed slaves and to publish the pro-suffrage *Free Enquirer* newspaper.

ZITKÁLA-ŠÁ, 1876–1938, YANKTON SIOUX OF SOUTH DAKOTA: author and cofounder of the National Council of American Indians. She advocated for suffrage for women and Native people. She is also known by her English name, Gertrude Simmons Bonnin.

1920 vs. 2020:
WOMEN BY THE NUMBERS

It was never *just* about the vote. Having a voice in politics was only the beginning, and once women could vote, they used that power to speak up, take charge, and demand equal treatment in other areas, too. They advocated for such laws as Title IX, which helped secure more equal treatment and resources for women in areas like education and sports, and they fought for rights like equal pay and access to credit. From the science lab to the soccer field to the Supreme Court, in the hundred years since the Nineteenth Amendment became law, women have stepped up and made their mark.

Let's run the numbers to see how women's positions have changed in the century since suffrage opened the floodgates.

Members of Congress: 1 in 1920 vs. 366 cumulative as of 2020

Representative Jeannette Rankin became the first woman elected to Congress in 1916—four years before women could vote nationwide. She was a Republican from Montana, one of the states where women had won the right to vote before the Nineteenth Amendment. As of the writing of this book, there are a record 131 women serving in Congress: 107 Democrats and 24 Republicans.

Supreme Court justices: 0 vs. 4

In 1981, Sandra Day O'Connor became the first woman to serve on the nation's highest court. As of the writing of this book, three of the nine justices are women: Ruth Bader Ginsburg, Elena Kagan, and Sonia Sotomayor.

US ambassadors: 0 vs. more than 450

Eugenie M. Anderson became the first American woman appointed as a US ambassador when President Harry Truman sent her to Denmark in 1949. Still, although progress has been made, only about one in four US ambassadors are women as of the writing of this book.

Bachelor's degrees awarded to women: 34 percent vs. 57 percent

The suffragists realized early on that access to education was a key part of women's treatment as equal members of society. One of the complaints against men in the Declaration of Sentiments, the document written at the Seneca Falls Convention in 1848, was that they had denied women "the facilities for obtaining a thorough education—all colleges being closed against her." As of 2020, more than half of US college graduates are women.

Doctors in the United States who are women: 5 percent vs. 36 percent

In 1849, Elizabeth Blackwell became the first American woman to graduate from medical school. By the 1920s, roughly 3 percent of medical students were female, and there was one medical school in the entire United States for women only. As of 2020, female medical students outnumber their male classmates—and they have hundreds of schools to choose from.

Nobel Prize winners: 4 vs. 53

Marie Curie, a Polish and French woman, became the first woman to win a Nobel Prize, for physics, in 1903. The first American woman to claim the honor was the social worker—and suffragist—Jane Addams, who won the peace prize in 1931. (Unfortunately, there's still a long way to go: over the last five years, women have made up only about 10 percent of all winners.)

Olympic athletes: 176 vs. 49,812

Women first participated in the modern Olympics in 1900. At the Tokyo Games, scheduled for 2021 as of the writing of this book, 49 percent of the athletes are expected to be women—the most yet.

US vice presidents: 0 vs. 0 and US presidents: 0 vs. 0

In 1964, Senator Margaret Chase Smith of Maine declared her candidacy in the Republican Party's presidential primary, making her the first woman to seek the nomination from a major political party. Representative Shirley Chisholm of New York was the first female Democrat—and the first African American from a major party—to do the same, in 1972. Hillary Clinton became the first female major-party nominee for the presidency when she won the Democratic primary in 2016, and there have been two women—Geraldine Ferraro, a Democrat, and Sarah Palin, a Republican—nominated by a major party for the vice presidency. But as of the writing of this book, no woman has been elected to either of the two highest offices in the United States.

★ SUFFRAGE FOREST ★

In the spring of 1919, as a constitutional suffrage amendment finally seemed within reach, Carrie Chapman Catt and her partner, Mary Garrett Hay, were ready for a much-needed break. They bought a farm in Westchester County, close enough to New York City that they could still be involved in the fight for women's rights but far enough away that they could get some space. Juniper Ledge was "isolated, quiet, restful, and gives promise of fun," Carrie wrote. And it offered a canvas on which to commemorate the long, hard decades of work that had brought the women to this point.

Carrie commissioned a series of twelve metal plaques honoring the leaders of the suffrage movement, from Susan B. Anthony and Elizabeth Cady Stanton to Dr. Anna Howard Shaw and Lucy Stone. She affixed the plaques to trees around the property, creating a path that wound from the cow pasture over the brook and through history. This suffrage forest was a living testament to the women who had devoted their lives to fighting for equality and voting rights—not only in the United States but around the globe. In 1922, the League of Women Voters of New York City commissioned one final plaque—to honor Carrie herself.

As these pages show, the work of suffrage did not end with the ratification of the Nineteenth Amendment. The fight to ensure the equal treatment of all people, regardless of gender, continues to this day. And as we continue this struggle, there are also women—historians, authors, curators, journalists—who have worked to preserve its history and to examine and expand our understanding of the suffrage movement. Many of these women met with us, answered our questions, and provided insight as we researched this book. We wanted to end it with our own suffrage forest as a tribute to them and their work.

ERICA ARMSTRONG DUNBAR
historian, author, and professor at Rutgers University

ELLEN CAROL DuBOIS
historian, author, and professor emerita at UCLA

TINA CASSIDY
author

KATE CLARKE LEMAY
historian and curator at the Smithsonian Institution's National Portrait Gallery

MARTHA S. JONES
historian, author, and professor at Johns Hopkins University

NELL IRVIN PAINTER
historian, author, and professor emerita at Princeton University

SALLY ROESCH WAGNER
historian, author, and founder of the Matilda Joslyn Gage Foundation

ADELE LOGAN ALEXANDER
historian, author, and granddaughter of the suffragist Adella Hunt Logan

ELAINE WEISS
journalist and author

SUSAN WARE
historian and biographer

ACKNOWLEDGMENTS

Like the suffrage movement, this book was a team effort that would not have been possible without the hard work and collaboration of many. We would like to thank the archival storytelling team at The New York Times, who were tireless in their efforts to help us put this book together. Thank you to Brian Thomas Gallagher, our senior staff editor; Nick Donofrio, our researcher; and Anika Burgess, our photo editor.

It was a very happy day in our offices when we got on the phone with Kwame Alexander and his talented team at Versify. Thank you, Kwame, for inspiring us with your vision and creativity. Our deepest thanks to our editors, Margaret Raymo and Erika Turner, as well as to our art director, Whitney Leader-Picone, and our designer, Ellen Duda. We are also grateful to the extended team at HMH, including Mary Magrisso, the managing editor; Tara Shanahan and John Sellers in publicity; Erika West and Maxine Bartow, who copyedited; and Susan Bishansky, who proofread.

We'd also like to thank Ellen Archer, president of HMH, who is both an old friend and the best cheerleader an author could have. Thank you as well to our agents, Kim Witherspoon and Jessica Mileo, who skillfully made the match with Versify.

The illustrators who worked on the portraits in this book wowed us with their energy and creativity. Thanks to Monica Ahanonu, Rachelle Baker, Kristen Buchholz, Alex Cabal, Noa Denmon, Shyama Golden, Johnalynn Holland, Hillary Kempenich, Nhung Lê, and Ella Trujillo. And a special shout-out to Steffi Walthall, who created a cover that is the embodiment of #squadgoals.

Laura Bullard and Lovia Gyarkye provided valuable fact-checking. Other New York Times team members offered insight and support, including Nakyung Han, Lorne Manly, Elizabeth Weinstein, Ari Isaacman Bevacqua, Jordan Cohen, Heidi Giovine, Heather Phillips, Lee Riffaterre, Amanda Cordero, Steve Brown, Jessica

White, Kelly Doe, Jason Fujikuni, Valencia Prashad, Jessica Bennett, Sharon Attia, Megan Kaesshaefer, and Francesca Donner.

We could not have made this book without the contributions of scholars, journalists, historians, and curators who have made suffrage, women's rights, and voting rights their life's work. Thank you to Adele Logan Alexander, Tina Cassidy, Erica Armstrong Dunbar, Kate Clarke Lemay, Sally Roesch Wagner, and Elaine Weiss for answering a million questions with patience and enthusiasm. A special thanks to Susan Ware, who read an early draft of this manuscript and generously gave us notes.

We sent out a questionnaire early on asking historians and scholars to share their expertise on the stories we wanted to tell. Our gratitude for answering those questions—and for consulting with us as we put the book together—goes to Martha S. Jones, Ellen Carol DuBois, Nell Irvin Painter, Jean H. Baker, Lori Ginzberg, Rebecca Mead, Robyn Muncy, and Cathleen D. Cahill. For their assistance, we would also like to thank Ann D. Gordon, Cynthia E. Orozco, Rachel Gunter, Louise Herne, Gabriela González, Vilma Martínez, Judith Wellman, Paul Ortiz, Carolivia Herron, Maureen Honey, and Charlotte Brooks.

You can't spend months studying the history of the suffrage movement without gaining a new appreciation for the grit and gumption it takes to be a powerful woman leader. We were lucky and thankful to have two of the most amazing women in the New York Times newsroom serve as our bosses on this project. Thank you to Monica Drake, assistant managing editor, and Caroline Que, editorial director for book development, for saying "yes" and "keep going!" when we needed to hear it most.

ILLUSTRATOR'S NOTE

This book is filled with remarkable women who worked to make suffrage a reality. I wanted the design of the book to reflect their diversity, complexity, and strength. For each chapter, I chose flowers and plants that were symbolic, holding deeper meanings. —Ellen Duda

CHAPTER ONE: Eastern white pine needles and cones. The white pine is a symbol of unity for the Haudenosaunee Confederacy. The needles grow in clusters of five, representing the five tribes unifying in peace.

CHAPTER TWO: yellow and "black" roses. Yellow roses, which symbolize hope, were worn at marches—and at the 1920 ratification vote in Tennessee—to communicate support for the suffrage movement. The "black" rose—in actuality, a red rose so dark it appears black—was promoted by Mary McCleod Bethune as a symbol of the importance of black women's inclusion in the fight for equality.

CHAPTER THREE: forest leaves of Pennsylvania. These leaves found in the woods of Frances's home state also recall her first published book of poetry, *Forest Leaves*.

CHAPTER FOUR: gladiolas. The gladiola symbolizes strength and moral integrity.

CHAPTER FIVE: Rocky Mountain columbine. In addition to being the state flower of Colorado, the columbine flower is a historical symbol of victory.

CHAPTER SIX: begonias. Begonias symbolize knowledge, deep thought, and harmonious communication.

CHAPTER SEVEN: violets. Violets have been a symbol for gay women since the poet Sappho wrote about them in ancient Greece. They were repopularized in 1926 by Édouard Bourdet's play *The Captive*, which featured a lesbian romance and included a scene where one of the women gave her partner a bouquet of the purple blooms.

CHAPTER EIGHT: plum blossoms. These flowers, which bloom in midwinter, symbolize perseverance and hope, and are very important in Chinese culture.

CHAPTER NINE: black-eyed Susans. In the Victorian era, hardy black-eyed Susans, which grow back year after year, came to symbolize justice.

CHAPTER TEN: dahlias. The dahlia is the national flower of Mexico and a symbol of inner strength and standing strong in your values.

CHAPTER ELEVEN: Tennessee coneflowers. This wildflower is native to Tennessee. Like the other echinacea flowers, it represents strength and healing.

CHAPTER TWELVE: goldenrods. In addition to being the state flower of Nebraska, the goldenrod is significant to the Omaha tribe. It was valued for its medicinal properties, and its blooms were a sign that the tribe's corn crops were almost ready to harvest.

CHAPTER THIRTEEN: prairie sage. This medicinal and ceremonial herb is very important to the Dakota tribe. It is traditionally braided into bracelets and crowns for dancers performing the sacred ceremonies featured in Zitkála-Šá's *The Sun Dance Opera*.

Further Reading

If you liked this book and want to read more stories about brave, remarkable women and people standing up for their rights, here are a few you might enjoy.

Bad Girls Throughout History: 100 Remarkable Women Who Changed the World by Ann Shen (Chronicle Books, 2016)

Bold & Brave: Ten Heroes Who Won Women the Right to Vote by Kirsten Gillibrand, illustrated by Maira Kalman (Knopf, 2018)

Bygone Badass Broads: 52 Forgotten Women Who Changed the World by Mackenzi Lee, illustrated by Petra Eriksson (Abrams, 2018)

Fearless Females: The Fight for Freedom, Equality, and Sisterhood by Marta Breen (Yellow Jacket, 2019)

Here We Are: Feminism for the Real World, edited by Kelly Jensen (Algonquin, 2017)

An Indigenous Peoples' History of the United States for Young People by Roxanne Dunbar-Ortiz (Beacon Press, 2019)

Little Leaders: Bold Women in Black History by Vashti Harrison (Little, Brown, 2017)

Make Trouble, Young Readers Edition: Standing Up, Speaking Out, and Finding the Courage to Lead by Cecile Richards with Lauren Peterson, adapted by Ruby Shamir (Margaret K. McElderry Books, 2019)

March by John Lewis and Andrew Aydin, illustrated by Nate Powell (Top Shelf Productions, 2013)

Notorious RBG: The Life and Times of Ruth Bader Ginsburg by Irin Carmon and Shana Knizhnik (Dey Street Books, 2015)

Rad American Women A-Z: Rebels, Trailblazers, and Visionaries Who Shaped Our History … and Our Future! by Kate Schatz, illustrated by Miriam Klein Stahl (City Lights Books, 2015)

Resist: 35 Profiles of Ordinary People Who Rose Up Against Tyranny and Injustice by Veronica Chambers (HarperCollins, 2018)

She Came to Slay: The Life and Times of Harriet Tubman by Erica Armstrong Dunbar (37 Ink, 2019)

Suffragette: The Battle for Equality by David Roberts (Walker Books, 2019)

The Women's Suffrage Movement, edited by Sally Roesch Wagner (Penguin Classics, 2019)

Photo Credits

Frontispiece (clockwise from top left) - New York State Library, Manuscripts and Special Collections, Albany, New York; National Woman Suffrage Publishing Co., Museum of the City of New York, 47.225.16; State Archives of Florida; National Museum of American History, Smithsonian Institution; Library of Congress; Collection of the Smithsonian National Museum of African American History and Culture

Introduction: This is What Suffrage Looks Like - Chicago History Museum/Getty Images (p. 1); Ken Florey Suffrage Collection/Gado/Getty Images (p. 3)

Chapter One: The Haudenosaunee Model - Private Collection/Courtesy of Sotheby's (p. 4); Bettmann/Getty Images (p. 6); Library of Congress (p. 9); Private Collection/Courtesy of Sotheby's (p. 10)

Chapter Two: How Bias Nearly Ruined the Suffrage Movement - Library of Congress (pp. 12, 16)

Chapter Three: Frances Ellen Watkins Harper: Lifting Up Her Voice - Library of Congress (p. 20); Maryland Historical Society, MP3.H284F (p. 21); New York State Library, Manuscripts and Special Collections, Albany, New York (p. 23)

Chapter Four: Josephine St. Pierre Ruffin: Spreading the Word - Buyenlarge/Getty Images (p. 28); Museum of African American History, Boston and Nantucket, USA (p. 31); George Rinhart/Corbis/Getty Images (p. 32)

Chapter Five: Elizabeth Piper Ensley Goes West - Library of Congress (p. 36); Dovie Horvitz Digital Collection/University of Wisconsin (p. 37)

Chapter Six: Mary Church Terrell and the Power of Language - Library of Congress (p. 42); Collection of the Smithsonian National Museum of African American History and Culture, Gift of Ray and Jean Langston in memory of Mary Church and Robert Terrell (p. 43); Afro American Newspapers/Gado/Getty Images (p. 45)

Chapter Seven: Angelina Weld Grimké, Mary Burrill, and the Queer Leaders of the Suffrage Movement - New York Public Library (p. 48); Courtesy of the Moorland-Spingarn Research Center, Manuscript Division, Washington, DC (p. 49); Library of Congress, Manuscript Division, Carrie Chapman Catt Papers (p. 51)

Sidebar: Suit Yourself - Corbis/Getty Images (p. 52); Library of Congress/Corbis/VCG/Getty Images (p. 53)

Chapter Eight: Mabel Ping-Hua Lee's Great Parade - Library of Congress (p. 56); The New York Times (p. 57); Schlesinger Library, Radcliffe Institute, Harvard University (p. 58); © 2020 The New York Times Company (p. 59)

Chapter Nine: Ida B. Wells-Barnett: Marching Forward - Library of Congress (p. 62); National Portrait Gallery, Smithsonian Institution (p. 63); Library of Congress (p. 65); Special Collections Research Center, University of Chicago Library (p. 66)

Sidebar: From Movement to Revolution - PA Images (p. 67); Hulton Archive/Getty Images (p. 68); National Archives, Photo No. 533773 (p. 70); Museum of London/Heritage Images/Getty Images (p. 71)

Chapter Ten: Jovita Idár: *El voto para las mujeres* - 084-0592, General Photograph Collection, UTSA Special Collections (p. 74); Library of Congress (p. 76); Women's Suffrage Collection, Ella Strong Denison Library, Scripps College (p. 78)

Chapter Eleven: Juno Frankie Pierce: A Square Deal or No Deal - Ken Florey Suffrage Collection/Gado/Getty Images (p. 84); Shawshots/Alamy (p. 87)

Chapter Twelve: Susette La Flesche Tibbles: Speaking Up for Her People - National Portrait Gallery, Smithsonian Institution (p. 90); History Nebraska (p. 92)

Chapter Thirteen: Zitkála-Šá Opens the Door - Corbis/Getty Images (p. 96); National Museum of American History, Smithsonian Institution (p. 97); Amherst College Archives & Special Collections (2) (p. 98)

Conclusion: Finish the Fight - Library of Congress (p. 100); History Nebraska (p. 101); State Archives of Florida (p. 103); Bettmann/Getty Images (p. 104); Bettmann/Getty Images (p. 105)

Authors' Note - National Museum of American History, Smithsonian Institution (p. 106)

Timeline - Beinecke Rare Book and Manuscript Library, Yale University (p. 108); National Park Service (p. 108); Everett Collection Inc/Alamy (p. 109); PhotoQuest/Getty Images (p. 110); Bettmann/Getty Images (p. 110); National Woman Suffrage Publishing Co., Museum of the City of New York, 47.225.16 (p. 111); William J. Smith/Associated Press (p. 111)

1920 v. 2020: Women by the Numbers - Ken Florey Suffrage Collection/Gado/Getty Images (p. 118)

Selected Bibliography

This is a partial list of our sources, which we hope will be useful to parents, teachers, and librarians. URLs accompany sources that were freely available online at the time of writing. We relied on numerous webpages maintained by the National Park Service, the Library of Congress, the Schlesinger Library at Harvard University, the Social Welfare History Project at Virginia Commonwealth University, the Emory Women Writers Resource Project, and the Archives of Women's Political Communication at Iowa State University. Britannica Academic was a general reference.

Alexander, Adele Logan. *Princess of the Hither Isles: A Black Suffragist's Story from the Jim Crow South*. New Haven, CT: Yale University Press, 2019.

"A Noted Indian Woman Dead." *New York Times,* Mar. 21, 1892.

Astor, Maggie. "In North Dakota, Native Americans Try to Turn an ID Law to Their Advantage." *New York Times,* Oct. 30, 2018. www.nytimes.com/2018/10/30/us/politics/north-dakota-voter-id.html.

Berkin, Carol, Christopher Miller, Robert Cherny, and James Gormly. *Making America: A History of the United States, Volume I: To 1877.* Boston: Cengage Learning, 2014.

Brooks, Charlotte. *American Exodus: Second-Generation Chinese Americans in China, 1901–1949.* Oakland: University of California Press, 2019.

Brown, DeNeen L. "Civil Rights Crusader Fannie Lou Hamer Defied Men—and Presidents—Who Tried to Silence Her." *Washington Post,* Oct. 6, 2017. www.washingtonpost.com/news/retropolis/wp/2017/10/06/civil-rights-crusader-fannie-lou-hamer-defied-men-and-presidents-who-tried-to-silence-her.

Bucy, Carol Stanford. "Juno Frankie Pierce." Tennessee Encyclopedia. Oct. 8, 2017. tennesseeencyclopedia.net/entries/juno-frankie-pierce.

Burn, Phoebe. Letter to Harry Burn from Mother. August 1920. Harry T. Burn Papers. Calvin M. McClung Historical Collection, Knox County Public Library. cmdc.knoxlib.org/cdm/ref/collection/p265301coll8/id/699.

Carrie Chapman Catt Center, Iowa State University. Archives of Women's Political Communication. awpc.cattcenter.iastate.edu. Accessed Apr. 24, 2020.

Cassidy, Tina. *Mr. President, How Long Must We Wait?: Alice Paul, Woodrow Wilson, and the Fight for the Right to Vote.* New York: 37 Ink, 2019.

Cooper, Brittney C. *Beyond Respectability: The Intellectual Thought of Race Women.* Urbana: University of Illinois Press, 2017.

Dando-Collins, Stephen. *Standing Bear Is a Person: The True Story of a Native American's Quest for Justice.* Boston: Da Capo, 2004.

DuBois, Ellen Carol. *Suffrage: Women's Long Battle for the Vote.* New York: Simon & Schuster, 2020.

Dunbar, Erica Armstrong. *A Fragile Freedom: African American Women and Emancipation in the Antebellum City.* New Haven, CT: Yale University Press, 2011.

Emory Women Writers Resource Project, Lewis H. Beck Center, Emory University. Women's Advocacy Collection. womenwriters.digitalscholarship.emory.edu/advocacy. Accessed Apr. 24, 2020.

Equal Rights Amendment. "History of the Equal Rights Amendment." www.equalrightsamendment.org/the-equal-rights-amendment. Accessed Apr. 24, 2020.

Flexner, Eleanor, and Ellen Fitzpatrick. *Century of Struggle: The Woman's Rights Movement in the United States.* Enlarged ed. Cambridge, MA: Belknap Press, 1996.

Giddings, Paula J. Ida. *A Sword Among Lions: Ida B. Wells and the Campaign Against Lynching.* New York: Amistad, 2008.

González, Gabriela. "Jovita Idár: The Ideological Origins of a Transnational Advocate for *La Raza.*" In *Texas Women: Their Histories, Their Lives,* ed. Elizabeth Hayes Turner, Stephanie Cole, and Rebecca Sharpless. Athens: University of Georgia Press, 2015. 225–48.

Goodstein, Anita Shafer. "A Rare Alliance: African American and White Women in the Tennessee Elections of 1919 and 1920." *Journal of Southern History* 64, no. 2 (1998): 219–46. doi.org/10.2307/2587945.

Grant, Ulysses S. Special Message to the Senate and House of Representatives. Mar. 30, 1870. The American Presidency Project, University of California, Santa Barbara. www.presidency.ucsb.edu/node/204128.

"Harlem Women Organize." *New York Times,* Feb. 2, 1910.

Harper, Frances Ellen Watkins. *A Brighter Coming Day: A Frances Ellen Watkins Harper Reader,* ed. Frances Smith Foster. New York: Feminist Press, 1990.

———. *Iola Leroy, or Shadows Uplifted.* 3rd ed. Boston: James H. Earle, 1892. docsouth.unc.edu/southlit/harper/harper.html.

Haudenosaunee Confederacy. "Government." www.haudenosauneeconfederacy.com/government. Accessed Apr. 20, 2020.

Holler, Deborah R. "The Remarkable Caroline G. Parker Mountpleasant, Seneca Wolf Clan." *Western New York Heritage,* Spring 2011.

Honey, Maureen. *Aphrodite's Daughters: Three Modernist Poets of the Harlem Renaissance.* New Brunswick, NJ: Rutgers University Press, 2016.

Jones, Martha S. *All Bound Up Together: The Woman Question in African American Public Culture, 1830-1900.* Chapel Hill: University of North Carolina Press, 2009.

———. "How the Daughters and Granddaughters of Former Slaves Secured Voting Rights for All." *Smithsonian Magazine,* March 8, 2019. www.smithsonianmag.com/smithsonian-institution/how-daughters-and-granddaughters-former-slaves-secured-voting-rights-all-180971660.

Keyssar, Alexander. *The Right to Vote: The Contested History of Democracy in the United States.* Rev. ed. New York: Basic Books, 2009.

La Jeunesse, Marilyn. "Who Was Jovita Idár, the Radical Muckraking Mexican-American Journalist." *Teen Vogue,* Oct. 13, 2018. www.teenvogue.com/story/jovita-idar-radical-muckraking-mexican-american-journalist.

Lee, Mabel. "The Meaning of Woman Suffrage." *The Chinese Students' Monthly* 9, no. 7 (May 1914): 526–31. books.google.com/books?id=3WkjAQAAIAAJ.

Lemay, Kate Clarke, ed. *Votes for Women: A Portrait of Persistence.* Princeton, NJ: Princeton University Press, 2019.

Library of Congress. www.loc.gov.

Lineberry, Cate. "'I Wear My Own Clothes.'" *New York Times,* Dec. 2, 2013. opinionator.blogs.nytimes.com/2013/12/02/i-wear-my-own-clothes.

McArdle, Terence. "'Night of Terror': The Suffragists Who Were Beaten and Tortured for Seeking the Vote." *Washington Post,* Nov. 10, 2017. www.washingtonpost.com/news/retropolis/wp/2017/11/10/night-of-terror-the-suffragists-who-were-beaten-and-tortured-for-seeking-the-vote.

Mead, Rebecca. *How the Vote Was Won: Woman Suffrage in the Western United States, 1868–1914.* New York: New York University Press, 2004.

"Mink in Senate Race." *Honolulu Star-Bulletin,* Oct. 25, 1975.

Mitchell, Damon. "The People's Grocery Lynching, Memphis, Tennessee." JSTOR Daily. Jan. 24, 2018. daily.jstor.org/peoples-grocery-lynching.

National Park Service. www.nps.gov/index.htm.

Nebraska Studies. "Susette La Flesche Tibbles." www.nebraskastudies.org/1875-1899/the-trial-of-standing-bear/susette-la-flesche-tibbles. Accessed Apr. 15, 2020.

Ortiz, Paul. *Emancipation Betrayed: The Hidden History of Black Organizing and White Violence in Florida from Reconstruction to the Bloody Election of 1920.* Berkeley: University of California Press, 2005.

Painter, Nell Irvin. *Sojourner Truth: A Life, a Symbol.* New York: W. W. Norton & Company, 1997.

Pankhurst, Emmeline. *My Own Story.* New York: Hearst's International Library, 1914. www.gutenberg.org/files/34856/34856-h/34856-h.htm.

Robinson, Marcia C. "The Tragedy of Edward 'Ned' Davis: Entrepreneurial Fraud in Maryland in the Wake of the 1850 Fugitive Slave Law." *Pennsylvania Magazine of History and Biography* 140, no. 2 (2016): 167–82.

Ruffin, Josephine St. Pierre. "Trust the Women!" *The Crisis,* August 1915. books.google.com/books?id=MAIcSWRw5ggC.

Ruiz, Vicki L. "Class Acts: Latina Feminist Traditions, 1900–1930." *American Historical Review* 121, no. 1 (Feb. 1, 2016): 1–16. doi.org/10.1093/ahr/121.1.1.

———. *From Out of the Shadows: Mexican Women in Twentieth-Century America.* 10th anniversary ed. Oxford: Oxford University Press, 2008.

Schechter, Patricia A. *Ida B. Wells-Barnett and American Reform, 1880–1930.* Chapel Hill: University of North Carolina Press, 2003.

Schlesinger Library on the History of Women in America, Radcliffe Institute for Advanced Study, Harvard University. Women's Suffrage Research Guide. guides.library.harvard.edu/ schlesinger/suffrage. Accessed Apr. 24, 2020.

Schmidt, Samantha. "This Pioneering Howard Dean Lived with Another Woman in the 1930s. Were They Lovers?" *Washington Post,* March 26, 2019. www.washingtonpost.com/his tory/2019/03/26/this-pioneering-howard-dean-lived-with-an other-woman-s-were-they-lovers.

Schuessler, Jennifer. "On the Trail of America's First Women to Vote." *New York Times,* Feb. 24, 2020. www.nytimes. com/2020/02/24/arts/first-women-voters-new-jersey.html.

Stanton, Elizabeth Cady. "Elizabeth Cady Stanton and the Presidential Election." *National Citizen and Ballot Box,* Nov. 2, 1880.

Staples, Brent. "When the Suffrage Movement Sold Out to White Supremacy." *New York Times,* Feb. 2, 2019. www.nytimes. com/2019/02/02/opinion/sunday/women-voting-19th-amend ment-white-supremacy.html.

Starita, Joe. *"I Am a Man": Chief Standing Bear's Journey for Justice.* New York: St. Martin's Press, 2008.

Still, William. *The Underground Rail Road.* Philadelphia: Porter & Coates, 1872. books.google.com/books?id=8ANWAAAAcAAJ.

Streitmatter, Rodger. *Raising Her Voice: African-American Women Journalists Who Changed History.* Lexington: University Press of Kentucky, 2015.

Terborg-Penn, Rosalyn. *African American Women in the Struggle for the Vote, 1850–1920.* Bloomington: Indiana University Press, 1998.

Tetrault, Lisa. *The Myth of Seneca Falls: Memory and the Women's Suffrage Movement, 1848–1898.* Chapel Hill: University of North Carolina Press, 2014.

"Thousands Carry Lunches to Polls." *New York Times,* Nov. 3, 1920.

Tseng, Tim. "Asian American Legacy: Dr. Mabel Lee." Tim Tseng. Dec. 13, 2013. timtseng.net/2013/12/12/asian-american-leg acy-dr-mabel-lee.

U.S. ex Rel. Standing Bear v. Crook. 25 F. Cas. 695. D. Neb. 1879. casetext.com/case/us-ex-rel-standing-bear-v-crook.

"Valuable Citizen." *Washington Post,* Sept. 23, 1953.

"Vast Suffrage Host Is on Parade To-Day." *New York Times,* May 4, 1912.

Virginia Commonwealth University Libraries. Social Welfare History Project. socialwelfare.library.vcu.edu. Accessed Apr. 24, 2020.

Wagner, Sally Roesch. "Feminism, Native American Influences." In *Encyclopedia of American Indian History,* ed. Bruce E. Johnson and Barry M. Pritzker. Santa Barbara, CA: ABC-CLIO, 2008. 383–88.

———. *Sisters in Spirit: Haudenosaunee (Iroquois) Influence on Early American Feminists.* Summertown, TN: Native Voices, 2011.

———, ed. *The Women's Suffrage Movement.* New York: Penguin, 2019.

Ware, Susan. *Why They Marched: Untold Stories of the Women Who Fought for the Right to Vote.* Cambridge, MA: Harvard University Press, 2019.

Wellman, Judith. *The Road to Seneca Falls: Elizabeth Cady Stanton and the First Woman's Rights Convention.* Urbana: University of Illinois Press, 2004.

Wells, Ida B. *The Light of Truth: Writings of an Anti-Lynching Crusader.* New York: Penguin, 2014.

Weiss, Elaine. *The Woman's Hour: The Great Fight to Win the Vote.* New York: Penguin, 2019.

"Women Get Election News." *New York Times,* Nov. 3, 1920.

Yellin, Carol Lynn, and Janann Sherman. *The Perfect 36: Tennessee Delivers Woman Suffrage,* ed. Ilene Jones-Cornwell. Oak Ridge, TN: Iris Press, 1998.

Zitkála-Šá. *American Indian Stories.* Washington, DC: Hayworth Publishing House, 1921. archive.org/details/americanindian s101zitk.

———. *Old Indian Legends.* Boston: Ginn & Company, 1902. cata log.hathitrust.rg/Record/006523059.

INDEX

A

abolitionist movement, 6, 22
Addams, Jane, 119
African Americans. *See also* civil rights movement; racism in the suffrage movement
    abolitionist movement, 6, 22
    lack of voting rights, 14–15, 17
    segregation, 17, 29, 43–44, 103
    slavery, 6, 13, 21–22, 41
    in suffrage movement, 17, 19–20, 31–32, 37, 66
Alpha Suffrage Club, 66
American Association of Educators of Colored Youth, 24
American Equal Rights Association (AERA), 109
Ames, Blanche Ames, 112
Anderson, Eugenie M., 118
Anthony, Lucy, 50
Anthony, Susan B.
    arrested for voting attempt, 16
    bio, 112
    first petition signed by, 14
    romantic relationships, 50
"Anthony Amendment," 2
Anti-Slavery Society of Maine, 22
Arizona, 110
Arkansas, 111

B

Baldwin, Marie Louise Bottineau, 112
Belmont, Alva Vanderbilt, 71
Bethune, Mary McLeod, 102, 112
Blackwell, Elizabeth, 119
Bloomer, Amelia, 28, 112
Bonnin, Gertrude Simmons. *See* Zitkála-Šá
Britain, suffrage movement in, 67–68
Brooks, Charlotte, 58
Brooks, Virginia, 62, 66
Brown, Mary Olney, 15
Burn, Harry T., 87
Burns, Lucy, 61, 68, 69
Burrill, Mary, 47–49, 112
Burroughs, Nannie Helen, 17

C

Capetillo, Luisa, 76
Cary, Mary Ann Shadd, 16, 17, 113

Catt, Carrie Chapman
    bio, 113
    honored in suffrage forest, 120
    relationship with Mary Garrett Hay, 50–51
    role in Colorado suffragist movement, 37
    role in NAWSA, 50, 69
Chinese Christian Center, 59
Chinese Exclusion Act (1882), 56–57, 59, 103
Chisholm, Shirley, 3, 119
Church, Robert, 42
civil rights movement. *See also* abolitionist movement; segregation; slavery
    American Association of Educators of Colored Youth, 24
    collaboration with white suffragists, 84, 85, 86
    Fifteenth Amendment, 14–15
    NAACP, 33, 65–66
    Nashville Federation of Colored Women's Clubs, 84
    National Association of Colored Women, 24
    1950s and 1960s, 103
Civil War, 13, 14, 52
Clinton, Hillary, 119
Coleman, Mattie E., 85, 113
Colorado, 37, 109
Colorado Federation of Women's Clubs, 38
Colorado Non-Partisan Equal Suffrage Association, 37
Colored Women's Progressive Franchise, 17
Constitution, 14, 43–44, 77, 83
Cook, Coralie Franklin, 113
Courant (newspaper), 30
Crisis (magazine), 33
Curie, Marie, 119
custody rights, 6

D

Dakota Sioux, 95, 96
Davis, Paulina Kellogg Wright, 28
Declaration of Independence, 5, 14
Declaration of Sentiments, 5–7, 119
De Priest, Oscar, 66
Díaz, Porfirio, 73
divorce, 6
Douglass, Frederick, 7, 15, 22, 43
Dred Scott case, 29

E

Eaton, Cora Smith, 113
education, importance of, 119
Election Day, 1920, 101
El Progreso, 73
Emancipation Proclamation, 13
Ensley, Elizabeth Piper
    activism, 36–38
    bio, 113
    early career, 36
    fight for racial equality, 17
    journalism, 30, 36–37
Equal Rights Amendment, 111
Equal Rights Party, 16
Equal Suffrage League of Brooklyn, 17
Evolución, 75

F

Ferraro, Geraldine, 119
Fifteenth Amendment, 14, 15
First Mexicanist Congress, 76
Fourteenth Amendment, 14
French, Charlotte Olney, 15

G

Gage, Matilda Joslyn, 8–9, 114
Ga-hah-no. *See* Mountpleasant, Caroline Parker"
Garnet, Sarah, 17
General Federation of Women's Clubs, 30–32
Ginsburg, Ruth Bader, 118
Grimké, Angelina Weld, 47–48, 114

H

Hamer, Fannie Lou, 103–4
Harper, Fenton, 22
Harper, Frances Ellen Watkins
    activism, 22–24
    bio, 114
    early career, 21–22
    fight for racial equality in, 17
    streetcar protest, 19
    upbringing, 20–21
Haudenosaunee
    cultural pressures faced by, 9–10
    society, 7–8, 11
    territory, 7
Haverfield, Evelina, 114
Hay, Mary Garrett, 50–51, 114, 120